Rebecca Greenwood is a very experienced, effective deliverance minister. Here she shares her expertise on ministering to children trapped in bondages because Satan has tried to ruin their lives from a very young age. Her teachings and methodologies can be thoroughly trusted, and I long to see an army of ministers raised up to work in this needy area.

—Doris Wagner
Cofounder, International Society
of Deliverance Ministers

With the daily bombardment of darkness from entertainment via movies, video games, books, etc., and the generational curses most are unaware of, *Let Our Children Go* is a must-read book for parents and anyone who has a heart for children. God has given Rebecca Greenwood insight, knowledge, and keys to deliver your children from the enemy's grip. Take these powerful spiritual principles, apply them, and see your children soar in their destiny.

—Ché Ahn
Senior Pastor, HROCK Church, Pasadena, CA
President, Harvest International Ministry
International Chancellor, Wagner Leadership
Institute

Rebecca Greenwood is a practitioner of spiritual warfare principles. She doesn't just write about such things—she lives it! Our children in this nation are subject to levels of darkness that previous generations have never known. The Internet, texting, Facebook, YouTube, MySpace, drug culture, movies, and music are influencing our children often more than the average parent realizes. This book is a must-read for heads-up understanding on how to protect your children from the ancient demonic powers of this age. You won't be disappointed.

—Alice Smith
r Center, Houston, TX
www.eddieandalice.com

Becca Greenwood is not only a superb writer and communicator, but she is also a woman with great insight and discernment when it comes to dealing with the demonic. She is unwavering when it comes to staying on a biblical track. And she is a people person. Becca has keen understanding of what people need and how they can discover a Spirit-led solution. She has a passion to see people walk in their God-given freedom. *Let My Children Go* is a usable, practical, and biblical approach to helping parents bring their children into the liberty Christ intended. A must-read for every parent.

—PASTOR CHRIS HAYWARD
PRESIDENT, CLEANSING STREAM MINISTRIES

LET OUR CHILDREN GO

REBECCA GREENWOOD

CHARISMA
HOUSE

Most CHARISMA HOUSE BOOK GROUP products are available at special quantity discounts for bulk purchase for sales promotions, premiums, fundraising, and educational needs. For details, write Charisma House Book Group, 600 Rinehart Road, Lake Mary, Florida 32746, or telephone (407) 333-0600.

LET OUR CHILDREN GO by Rebecca Greenwood
Published by Charisma House
Charisma Media/Charisma House Book Group
600 Rinehart Road
Lake Mary, Florida 32746
www.charismahouse.com

Visit the author's website at www.christianharvestintl.org.

Library of Congress Cataloging-in-Publication Data:
Greenwood, Rebecca, 1967-
  Let our children go / Rebecca Greenwood.
      p. cm.
  Includes bibliographical references.
  ISBN 978-1-61638-258-2 (trade paper) -- ISBN 978-1-61638-568-2 (e-book)
  1. Christian education--Home training. 2. Christian education of children. 3.
Children--Religious life. 4. Spiritual warfare. 5. Demoniac possession. I. Title.
  BV1590.G74 2011
  248.8'45--dc23
                                        2011023047

11 12 13 14 15 — 9 8 7 6 5 4 3 2 1
Printed in the United States of America

I dedicate this book to Peter and Doris Wagner. It is an honor to be in relationship with you. I am blessed to be serving, aligned, and walking with you. I am forever grateful for those incredible years of the warfare prayer conferences, the deliverance conferences, and all the training you have brought and continue to bring to the body of Christ. For me personally, I have learned to have great faith, to believe God for the impossible, to see cities and nations changed through prayer, the captives set free, and to speak the prophetic word of the Lord with boldness. I have learned through your example how to never shrink back but to advance in passion, humility, and love. You are forerunning pioneers who impacted the world and the church. Thank you for loving me, believing in me, encouraging me, and imparting into me. I love you.

Acknowledgments

I CAN HONESTLY SAY that writing a book is a birthing process. While there are not the physical discomforts (thank You, Jesus!), there is definitely the creative pressure, the tension of having to pen the words on page, and the endless hours and late nights on the computer. There is much anticipation about the project, but the process requires a great amount of time. When you write, there are many who go through this journey as well. I want to take the time to recognize those who have walked through the path of assisting me and making it possible to pull all the pieces together for this book.

First, I want to say, "Thank You, Jesus," for guiding me and giving me the strength and grace to complete this book in the midst of a very intense travel schedule. I am still amazed at the supernatural involvement in the completion of this manuscript.

Second, I want to acknowledge my husband, Greg—for the tireless nights of reading what I have written and sharing me with a computer screen and this manuscript...for the times you had to take and pick up the girls from school...and all the cooked meals, washed laundry, and chores around the house you did while I wrote (you are a great dad!)...for running the office and making sure everything stays caught up...for all the sacrifices you have made throughout our twenty-three years of marriage and for the belief in the international ministry the Lord has called me to, I truly appreciate it all. I love you and believe it is your time to soar.

To my precious three girls: Kendall, Rebecca, and Katie. You are all young women of honesty and integrity. You amaze me. Thank you for sharing your mom with the nations and for bringing understanding and patience when I write. The input all three of you gave to this project is invaluable. Thank you for allowing me to share our spiritual journey in such transparency. You are the apple of my eye. I believe in you and love you all so dearly. God has great days and adventures ahead. And I say go further, farther, and higher than your dad and I ever have. You are blessed with all the spiritual blessings, love, and favor from our matchless, heavenly Father. And on a fun note, I say as a family we are all due a really awesome vacation during the holidays this year!

Sharon Tindell, I want to say a huge and warm thank-you. Words do not suffice how genuinely grateful I am for all your assistance! I want to give complete credit where credit is due. This dear friend is a powerful intercessor and what I term a research queen! For those of you reading this book, Sharon was the one who did all the extensive research on all the statistics and quotes throughout the manuscript. I mean it when I say she is the reason this book was completed. Personally, she is involved in advocating, speaking out, educating, and campaigning to see an end to the human sex trafficking industry. She is a righteous warrior contending for justice, a wonderful wife, a dedicated mother, and a forever friend. I love you!

Maureen Eha, thank you for believing in this book and the message it brings to the church and this next generation. This is a much-needed resource, and you were able to see it and say yes! I am grateful to you and Charisma House, and I pray we will have many writing partnerships ahead. You are a friend and a faithful woman of God. Abundant blessings to you, your family, and the Charisma House family.

To my faithful friend, Kate Larson: thank you for reading through every chapter, sharing what I missed and encouraging me in what to include. I am forever appreciative for your tireless support, encouragement, prayers, and honesty. You, Brandon, and Kaira are a part of us. I am honored to be lifelong friends. I am expectant of all the Lord has ordained, and I am certain that the best is yet ahead. It is going to be a wonderful kingdom adventure.

Brad and Kris Herman, we love you! Thank you for the invaluable counsel and advice, Brad, for helping me walk through all my book projects and the spot-on wisdom and guidance you always bring. And Kris, thank you for just always being there for me. It is a wonderful privilege to have such a dear friend who is available not only to me but also to my three girls. How much we cherish our relationship with you.

And to all of those who intercede for us and who carried me on your prayers during this writing time, I am indebted to you. I could not write, teach, pray, and impart into the nations without your faithful prayer support. From one intercessor to other intercessors, I speak blessings, love, increase, and a fresh touch of the Father's heart. You are all loved, sincerely appreciated, and prayed for.

Contents

Foreword

As one watches the media outlets of today, there is no doubt that people are hungry for reality. However, one of the most overlooked realities is that of the unseen realm. The Holy Spirit is once again bringing the truth behind spiritual reality to the forefront.

While the Word of God is clear that we do not battle against flesh and blood but against powers of darkness (Eph. 6:12), it seems that even those who give some kind of theological acquiescence have relegated this biblical reality to the back burner. In the meantime, we are trying every natural method to set people free from dark bondages without once taking a look at what is happening in the spiritual world.

As one looks around at the number of escalating teen suicide victims and the explosive violence among children, we need to wake up and be willing to look beyond the seen realm into the truths that the Bible has set before us concerning the need for casting out demons. There is a reason that Jesus taught His disciples to pray, "*Deliver us from evil,*" rather than, "Save me from my wrong mental impressions." Scripture tells us that demonic powers are as real an enemy to our well-being as any problem we might have in life.

While I do believe that we need Christian counselors, I also believe that I have a biblical case that many people will not be healed and made whole without breaking demonic bondages.

Through the years there have been excesses in spiritual warfare ministries. Many have gone to the extreme simply to exclude this kind of ministry from the church. It seems strange to me that this would be the case when there are those who misuse the pulpit as well, but we still need them and the people who stand behind them!

A good friend of mine once said to me, "Cindy, we go fishing for souls, and we don't clean the fish; they stink!" Probably more than a few pastors would say, "Well, I know that is right! I have a few that really stink up my church!"

For these reasons I read this book by Rebecca Greenwood with interest. Having written a whole book on the occult myself entitled aptly, *Deliver Us From Evil*, I learned a bit about this subject. Not only that, but also I am a practitioner who has seen remarkable results by praying for people to be set free in the manner Rebecca prescribes.

All this to say that from my viewpoint, Rebecca has written one of the most practical, user-friendly books on ministering to children and teens that I have ever seen. It is balanced in its approach and gives us step-by-step guidance on ministering to children in a nonthreatening manner that is not spiritually abusive.

I turned from page to page marveling at the relevance of the subjects Rebecca chose to include. She has taken on tough issues such as the issues of emo and cutting. (If you don't know what these are and you are a parent, you need to know.) Time and time again while I was teaching a youth conference with a largely Christian audience, the Holy Spirit would nudge me to make a call for young people who have been cutting. I have carried home "trophies" of their freedom in the form of knives. After I had ministered deliverance to one young teenage girl, she put a pocketknife in my hand that she had been using to cut herself since she was eight years old! This is one of the many reasons we need this book.

Another reason I like this book is that it is well researched. Rebecca pulls in the advice and counsel of others in her field. There is substance to what she writes about, both from her experience and that of other leaders.

Some of you reading this book may not have had the privilege of knowing Rebecca Greenwood as I do as a person. She lives this message, and the sweetness and love that come through page after page is real in her everyday life. As a friend, I can say she genuinely cares for people with Christ's love.

Let Our Children Go is destined to be a classic that you will want to keep in your library for the rest of your life. It will also be one that you want to send to every mother who is weeping over her children because of huge problems that cannot be simply counseled away; they need to be cast away!

—CINDY JACOBS
GENERALS INTERNATIONAL
DALLAS, TEXAS

Introduction

MY HEART BROKE as fourteen-year-old John fell to his knees, lowering his head and pleading, "Please pray for me, pastor. Please pray one more time!" The previous night I had prayed for him. It was obvious this young man was demonically tormented. He wept and desperately cried out to God to deliver him. Through prophetic revelation I felt that the cause of his bondage was due to abuse from his father. John and his pastor confirmed this to be true. He was so traumatized by this abuse that he was unable to sleep unless medicated. As I ministered the Father's love, the power of the Lord set him free. That night John was able to sleep through the night peacefully without medication.

The following evening as he asked for further prayer, we ministered again. John was elated as he received more freedom. However, I was torn to leave him. I knew he needed even more prayer in order to receive complete release from the strongholds. My flight left the following morning, and I would not be able to pray for him again. Making sure things were in order for John to receive the freedom the Lord had for him, I instructed the leaders on how to continue his ministry. As I left, I told the Lord, "We need leaders who know how to minister deliverance, inner healing, and the Father's heart to the next generation. The church has to know how to protect and free the next generation from the traps the enemy has set and our purpose in releasing them into destiny." The Lord replied, "Yes, Becca. This is needed. Why don't you begin to do the equipping?"

Our ministry receives many calls to minister to children. The normal statement is, "We understand you know how to pray for children and teenagers. We have not been able to find another ministry that has the understanding and ability to do this." Now I know there are others who have the knowledge and experience to minister deliverance to children, teenagers, and young adults, but they are few.

Statistics show that only 4 percent of this next generation will be involved in evangelical Christianity.[1] The church has to make many changes in order to reach this generation effectively. When John the Baptist was born, his father prophesied that he was destined to *turn the hearts of the fathers to the children* (Luke 1:17). We are living in a day and time where the love of the mothers and fathers to their children and spiritual mothers and fathers to their spiritual children is crucial. I believe a large portion of the struggle with this next generation is a spiritual battle. Darkness is on the rise, and it is the role of parents, youth pastors, pastors, and believers to do all we can to ensure the blessing, protection, and freedom of this younger generation, empowering them to reach their fullest kingdom destiny. It is my desire and belief that this book will be the equipping tool that the church, leaders, and believers can use to reach this goal.

Chapter 1

Demons Really Want to Harm My Child?

THE ANSWER IS yes. Demons really do want to harm our children. The greatest danger to children and adults comes from an unseen force. It is Satan and his army of darkness. This evil spiritual army is obsessed with and completely focused on keeping as many men, women, and children eternally separated from the love of God and the saving grace of Jesus. We must not assume that our children are not a threat to darkness. The enemy's purpose is to grip and blind every generation, establishing strongholds in the lives of our children from a very young age.

God created mankind because He has a Father's heart and He wanted children to love. Just as earthly fathers and mothers long to have children born out of loving relationship, our heavenly Father also yearns for relationship with us, His children. Therefore, from the time we are conceived, through birth and throughout our lives, the enemy will set up traps, snares, and schemes in order to keep us bound to lies of darkness and paralyzed from reaching our fullest kingdom potential. He is a predator looking to kill, steal, and destroy all that God wants to release in our lives.

A Modern-Day Story of Breaking the Power of a Deaf and Dumb Spirit

The distraught mother approached the altar with the lifeless two-year-old Henry in her arms. A feeding tube protruded from his little nose. His face was drastically swollen from all the medications. What should have been a happy, full-of-life little boy was a sick child ridden with seizures and barely alive. Cathy, his Chinese mother, in desperation to save her sick child, begged us to pray for him.

Speaking through her interpreter, I asked Cathy what was wrong with Henry. She explained that he had been suffering from seizures since birth. The doctors were unable to diagnose his condition. I asked, "There is no medical diagnosis for the seizures and sickness?" "No." Feeling a nudge from the Holy Spirit, I asked Cathy if they were Christians. "No, we are Hindu. We also worship Buddha and are involved in Taoism."

"Cathy, why did you come to this service today?"

"Because the Hindu priests, the Buddhist monks, and all the Taoist rituals have proven powerless to heal my son." She shared how they had taken him to every temple on the island for healing. Instead of Henry's condition being helped, it grew worse. The doctors had given no hope. The prognosis was a fast-approaching death.

I told Cathy we would pray for Henry, but first she needed our attention. I shared the message of salvation, and shortly after receiving the gift of eternal life, her countenance drastically changed. We asked if she felt the love of Jesus. With joyful tears she replied, "Yes, I do."

"Cathy, before I pray for Henry, you need to assure my friend Pam and me that you and your husband will no longer take Henry to these temples. Only Christians can lay hands on him. You have been asking demonic gods to bring healing to your son. The result has been more demons invading his body, causing his critical illness." I inquired if she and her husband had dedicated Henry at birth to dead ancestors and Hindu gods. She proudly responded, "Yes!"

We explained we were going to minister deliverance prayers. Cathy quickly agreed. We broke the power of all baby dedications to Hindu gods and dead ancestors. We commanded all witchcraft, anti-Christ spirits, spirits of infirmity, and death to go in the name of Jesus. I commanded, "Deaf and dumb spirit, I bind your power over Henry and his body right now in Jesus's name. I break your power and command you to go." Pam was praying in agreement.

Suddenly Henry's body grew rigid as he went into an intense seizure. His face turned blue from the lack of oxygen. I remember being very thankful that Pam was not only a powerful prayer warrior but also a gifted nurse. In agreement, we commanded that spirit to go and to loose Henry. This two-year-old opened his eyes, gasped for air, and his overly chubby cheeks turned pink. Something had changed. We spoke healing, freedom, and the anointing of the Holy Spirit into little Henry. Peace came on him. He was coming out of his slumber.

The following night Cathy, Henry, and her Hindu husband came to a Christian service for the first time as a family. She ran to the altar with Henry in her arms. She was so radically changed I almost did not recognize her. Cathy was elated. "My unsaved husband who wanted nothing to do with the Christian Jesus came with me tonight! I am filled with joy. Henry only had one minor seizure today. Only one!" I prayed for them again. We rejoiced in the Lord together.

That night the father went home and threw out every good luck charm and demon god attached to Hinduism, Taoism, and Buddhism. They took Henry to the hospital two days later for more scheduled tests. Everything came back normal. Henry had been seizure free for days. He was opening his eyes and growing more alert. The father told the hospital staff that only Christian pastors could pray for and touch their son. In the hospitals of their nation, Hindu priests make their daily routes to dedicate children to their gods. It was forbidden for any to come to Henry's room.

Since they could find nothing wrong with Henry, the doctors dismissed him from the hospital. Cathy, Henry, and the father began to regularly attend church. The father renounced his occult practices and received salvation. Henry is totally healed.

Our God is a miraculous, delivering, healing God! One little boy's intense battle with a stronghold of a deaf and dumb spirit led a family to seek the one true God. As a result, salvation, healing, and freedom flooded in. God can take what the enemy meant for terrible harm and turn it for good. Revival and a move of God can sweep through and ignite a family to be radical followers of Him.

History of Demonic Attacks Against the Next Generation

We have seen repeatedly throughout Bible history the attacks Satan has unleashed against children. Pregnant mothers were ripped open and their babies killed. Herod ordered the death of all male infants under the age of two. Throughout history there has been the annihilation and genocide of children—in the Spanish Inquisition, the Holocaust, and, in recent history, the genocide of children in Rwanda, Iraq, and many other nations. This is not to mention the horror of Muslim boys being trained to give their lives in jihad from six years of age and the murder of more than 40 million unborn babies that has occurred in our nation alone since 1973. Satan attempts to initiate his plans of destruction beginning at conception and continuing throughout our lives.

Nothing grieves me more than seeing a young child or teenager gripped by darkness and unable to function. Childhood should be a time of joy, laughter, playing, finding ourselves through the guidance of loving parents and a church full of the life of Jesus, and memories of special family times and holiday gatherings. During these years it is God's design for children to grow and thrive in a loving home atmosphere, to hear the message of salvation, and to grow in a spiritual relationship with Him.

One day we were driving in the car with our three daughters. Four-year-old Rebecca was quietly sitting in the back. It was obvious she was processing something in her little mind. She curiously asked, "Daddy, there is God and Jesus…and who is the other brother?" We laughed as she voiced her question but were thankful to hear her at such a young age pondering on our Father, Jesus, and the Holy Spirit and how they relate to one another. Unfortunately, there are many children who are never given this opportunity.

Pharaoh's Mandated Child Murder

There are many instances in the Bible where we witness the enemy unleashing his plans against the younger generation. We saw it in Egypt as Pharaoh ordered all the male newborns to be killed by the Hebrew midwives, Shiphrah and Puah. Praise God they were not obedient. As these women feared the Lord, they called on His name asking Him to cause the women to deliver before they arrived. Pharaoh was not impressed with their explanation. I am sure they did not tell him that they had prayed and God faithfully answered. However, he then began to initiate phase two of his plan.

All Egyptians were ordered to throw all the Israeli baby boys into the Nile River. (See Exodus 1:22.) Therefore child murder became a mandated and justifiable practice in Egypt. Idolatry, witchcraft, and divination were steeped in the beliefs and practices of ancient Egypt. Pharaoh's top advisors were experts in tapping into demonic powers to achieve supernatural strength. Satan was using Pharaoh and his advisors to implement his plan of wiping out the Hebrew nation to keep the favored child from coming forth. As we know, Pharaoh's plan was unsuccessful and ultimately brought the end result in which God said, "Let My son go, that he may serve Me; and if you refuse to let him go, behold, I will slay your son, your firstborn" (Exod. 4:23, AMP).

Child Sacrifice

While God required animal sacrifice in the Old Testament for atonement of sins, Satan required human sacrifice, his preferred choice being children. The pagan religious ceremonies of ancient civilizations were times of demonic worship. The worship surrounding both masculine and feminine deities was practiced with sexual perversion. Fertility rites, male and female temple prostitution, and sexual sin became a part of the ritualistic expression. The climax of this worship was the offering of children as sacrifices to the demonic deities. We read in 1 Kings 11:7–13 about King Solomon building altars to the gods of his wives, and specifically to Chemosh, the detestable god of Moab, and Molech, the detestable god of the Ammonites.

Molech, whose name means king, was the fire-god of the Ammonites and was essentially identical to the Moabite god Chemosh. According to tradition, the image of Molech was of brass and hollow within. His face was that of a calf, and his hands were outstretched like a man waiting to receive something. The priests would kindle the arms of the idol with fire, take a young baby, and put it into the hands of Molech, sacrificing the child to the demon god. While we consider this terrible and inhumane, the truth is, modern-day abortion is child sacrifice. It is the enemy's way of trying to stop the next generation.

Herod's Enraged Murder Plot

Herod was infamous for the murders he committed. When the Magi did not return to him with the directions on how to find the baby Jesus, he was furious. The enemy attempted to kill Jesus through an enraged Herod; he issued a death sentence to all boys two years old and younger. (See Matthew 2:16–18.)

The enemy has historically tried to unleash his schemes of death and destruction onto the younger generation. If he can halt the plans and purposes of God by attacking, harassing, causing crippling fear, and killing, he will do it.

My Story of Fear to Freedom

I am passionate about seeing this younger generation set free. I too was one whom the enemy tried to halt through fear and other traps. Fear was something I struggled with throughout my childhood years into early adulthood. When my sister and I were children, we were staying at a childcare facility while our parents went to a Dallas Cowboys football game. She was six years old; I was three. While climbing on the monkey bars, I fell and broke my elbow. Cell phones did not exist, so the caretaker was unable to reach my parents. I continued to cry uncontrollably.

Frustrated, she placed me in a crib in a dark room and refused to allow my distraught sister to comfort me. I vividly remember my sister standing in the doorway of the room wanting to come to me and not being allowed to do so. I was in pain and frightened. Needless to say, when my parents returned, they were not happy.

Because of that incident, I became terrified of heights and the dark. From that time until I was delivered from fear as an adult, I was plagued with nightmares. Even after Greg and I were married and had our first child, fear gripped me. If he was traveling out of town on business, I could not sleep unless the television, radio, and every light in the house were on. When I traveled by plane, I had to take enough Dramamine to put me to sleep. I could not stand ladders or balconies.

As the Lord began to teach me about intercession, deliverance, and warfare, I realized I had to deal with these fears. How could I cast out a spirit of fear in another individual if I was walking in fear? How could I go to the places and nations the Lord was revealing to me if I was afraid of flying? I began to cry out to Him for freedom. One time at a women's retreat, the speaker asked all of the women with fear issues to stand. He prayed over us corporately and broke the spirit of fear. I felt as if something perched on my shoulders left. I was thrilled!

When I returned home, I knew I had been set free. Even so I quickly learned that I was going to have to stand in my deliverance to keep the victory.

Every night for two months I dealt with a spirit of fear. I could feel when the spirit would enter our home while we slept. Instead of burrowing my head under the covers or scooting closer to my husband for comfort, I would get out of bed, walk to the family room, and address that spirit of fear. Even though I could not see it, I would walk to where I felt its presence and address it as if I were staring it in the eyes. I told it to leave in Jesus's name and never come back. It was no longer welcome in my life or home. I told fear that it would not touch my children or my husband.

During this time, I spent many late-night hours praying. Even when I was worshiping the Lord and moving into intercession, that spirit of fear attempted to return. I would rise from the floor and walk to the spot where I could feel that spirit and address it face-to-face.

Greg left town on a business trip. This was the true test! At night, after putting my daughter to bed, I turned off all the lights. The television and radio were off, and I proclaimed, "I am not submitting to fear any longer! I will not embrace you! Your assignment is over, and I say you will not come on me again or my children and their children and generations to come!" Guess what? I was not afraid! Since that time darkness and dark places do not bother me, and I have been able to fly without hesitation.

There is no need for our young to walk through their early years of life in fear, depression, harassment, or torment. Freedom does not have to wait until the adult years. This is the purpose of this book: to equip the church in how to minister to our young and provide a way for them to walk in victory from an early age.

Our Children and Teenagers Are Still at Risk Today

We would all agree that at our time in history darkness is alive and well. I do not say this to generate fear. Nor do I believe that Satan is as powerful as our Lord—absolutely not. But we live in a dark time in history, and the following statistics from the Teen Mania website prove that this is the case. This generation is in great need of the truth.

+ Ninety-one percent say there is no absolute truth.

+ Seventy-five percent of teens in America believe the central message of the Bible is, "God helps those who help themselves."

+ Fifty-three percent believe Jesus committed sin (40 percent of born-again teens believe Jesus committed sin).[1]

This younger generation is seeking. They are going to see, experience, and be a part of the most strategic and intense times in the history of the Christian church. They are going to witness firsthand amazing events unfold in our world and miraculous signs and wonders that even the prophets of the Bible wrote about. But there is a battle of darkness raging to keep them out of the light and in deception.

I love what Paul wrote to his spiritual son Timothy in 1 Timothy 6:11–14, 20, as he obviously knew the dangers that his spiritual son would face and instructed him on how to rise above the traps of the world and the enemy.

Paul exhorts Timothy to flee evil, including all the temptations of money and all the evils associated with it, to pursue righteousness and fight the good fight of faith. Reading these verses causes me to ponder. Our children, or those raised in the church, are normally taught to flee evil and to follow after righteousness. But I question how well we have done fighting on behalf of our youth and teaching them how to fight the good fight of faith.

The Greek word for *fight* in this scripture is *agonizimai*. It means "to enter a contest, to contend with adversaries, struggles and dangers." *Contend* means "to struggle in opposition"; "to wrestle, grapple, battle, fight, compete, argue, wrangle, hold and claim." Isn't this what we do in battles with our adversary? We wrestle in battle to fight the competition and struggle against all the arguments of darkness, disputing their hold and taking hold and claiming our freedom and inheritance in the kingdom of God.

Paul understood this. He told Timothy to keep the deposit entrusted to him. Friends, it is our responsibility to guard and keep what God has entrusted to us. We have to step into the knowledge of how to guard and keep not only for our personal lives but also for the lives of our children.

Train Up a Child

One of my favorite truths I teach is that knowledge builds power for action. Part of our role in raising the next generation is discovering who the child is and encouraging him to go that direction as stated in Proverbs 22:6: "Train up a child in the way he should go [and in keeping with his individual gift or bent], and when he is old he will not depart from it" (AMP).

Now more than ever we must ensure this younger generation is trained in the way God desires for them to go. We have to discover who each of them is called to be—not placing them into a cookie-cutter mold, but finding the individual anointing and calling and enabling them to pursue what they have been created for.

We are to have spiritual eyes, wisdom, and discernment to stop the schemes of darkness in their lives from a young age, therefore empowering them to be all they are to be. As we advance, it is my prayer that the instruction needed to deliver our children will be imparted and they will be released into victorious freedom as children of the King, ushering this next generation into kingdom destiny.

Prayer for Discernment

Lord, thank You that You are opening my spiritual eyes to see, understand, and discern the spiritual atmosphere in my life, home, and my children's lives. Give Your insight to the traps the enemy wants to unleash into the lives of my children. I welcome You, Holy Spirit, to enlighten the words in the pages of this book. Help me to see and know the schemes of the enemy, not only in my life but also in the life of this next generation. Cause me to be a sharp tool and weapon in Your hands to see those young ones who are trapped in darkness set free. I thank You that as I read these pages, I will have understanding of open doors in my life. Let this be a time of breaking through into freedom and a time of setting our feet on a sure foundation on a new path of understanding the things of the Spirit. Lord, give me Your heart and vision of freedom for my children and this next generation. I invite You to cause me to see and stand in my kingdom authority to see freedom released. In Jesus's name, amen.

Chapter 2

What on Earth Has Invaded Our Home?

OUR OLDEST DAUGHTER, Kendall, has always been content and slept through the night from the time she was five weeks of age. But one morning when she was two years old, around 3:00 a.m., my husband and I awoke from a dead sleep, hearing screaming coming from her room. We rushed to Kendall's room to console her and could not calm her unless we laid her in bed with us. This happened again the following night at the same exact time.

The next morning I called our pastor. I explained we needed a prayer team to come to our home. Something in our house was scaring Kendall. The pastor explained, "You do not need a prayer team. Your daughter is seeing things in the spirit realm." Being new to this, I questioned, "Seeing in the spirit realm?" He explained that many times children see things in the spiritual realm and are taught that what they are seeing is not real. It is just a bad dream or their imagination. He told us that when Kendall woke up afraid that night, to go into her room and ask, "'Sweetie, are you seeing something?' If she says yes, ask her if what she is seeing is good or bad. If she answers, 'Good,' she could be seeing an angel; even that can be scary when a child first begins to experience this. If she answers, 'Bad,' then you need to pray and demand, in Jesus's name, that it leave her room. Then you pray and ask God to send His angels of protection."

Needless to say, that night Greg and I tried to sleep, but it was difficult. We were tensely waiting for Kendall to wake up. I remember lying in bed thinking, "What on earth is happening in my home?" The longer I thought about it, the more I felt a righteous anger rise up in me. I did not like the thought of a demon trying to harm my baby! Just like clockwork at 3:00 a.m., she woke up screaming. We jumped out of

13

bed and nervously walked to her room. Yes, we were a little nervous; this was definitely a first for us too!

As we entered her room, she ran to us for comfort. We turned the light on and quizzed her as directed by our pastor. We asked, "Honey, are you seeing something?" She nervously answered, "Yes." We continued, "Is it good or bad?" She fearfully answered, "It is bad, Momma and Dadda. Bad! It is a big bad gorilla!" We then prayed and commanded that evil spirit to leave. We asked, "Is it gone?" "Yes," she quickly responded. We asked the Lord to send His angels to watch over and protect her. As soon as we finished praying, a smile broke out on our daughter's face. She exclaimed, "An angel, Momma and Dadda. It is so pretty!" We then placed her back in bed, and she peacefully drifted back to sleep. Greg and I left the room awed at what had just transpired.

The next night she woke up again screaming. We quickly walked to her room but were not as nervous this time. We asked her the same questions as we had the night before and received the same answers. But as we prayed this time, we placed Kendall between the two of us, holding her little hands. We instructed her to command that spirit to leave in Jesus's name, and then she asked God to send His angels of protection. Our daughter at the age of two prayed these prayers, and that demon obeyed her command and God sent His angels of protection in response to her request.

Since that time Kendall has been very sensitive to things in the spirit and has understood her authority in Jesus. She understands the scriptural truth of resisting the enemy. We can instruct our children to defend against evil.

Things That Are Unseen Are Real

In walking out this process with Kendall, we quickly realized that the spiritual realm is more real than the physical realm. What we see in the natural is temporal and will fade away, but the unseen realm is eternal and very active. Paul wrote in 2 Corinthians 4:18 (AMP):

Since we consider and look not to the things that are seen
but to the things that are unseen; for the things that are
visible are temporal (brief and fleeting), but the things that
are invisible are deathless and everlasting.

Many times we hear that our children are afraid of the dark, fearful
of what they see at night. They will refer to the monster or bad person
that visits during the night hours. These young ones are seeing in the
spirit realm, and they know that what they are seeing is real. One of
the most important things we can do is tell our children we believe
them when they say they are seeing something scary, even when our
adult eyes do not see it. The spiritual realm, which is alive, well, and
active, is real to our young. When we discourage our children and tell
them what they are seeing is not real, we are training them to shut
down their anointing as seers.

The story from 2 Kings is a powerful example of learning to see the
reality of the spirit realm. Elisha's servant with his physical eyes saw
only their city surrounded with the horses and chariots of the enemy
army there to arrest the prophet. The man of God prayed, "Lord, I
pray You, open his eyes that he may see" (2 Kings 6:17, AMP). As the
servant viewed the unseen realm, he discovered the Lord had placed
horses and chariots of fire all around the prophet to protect him. The
reality of the unseen world contained a greater army for Elisha than
the seen world held against him.

Paul talks further in 1 Corinthians 12:16–27 concerning how we
are part of the body but function in different roles. Some operate as
feet. There are those called to be the hands. Some are the eyes, and
some are the ears. Paul clearly explains we all need each other to make
up the body. God designed us this way. In my experience the children
who begin seeing or hearing in the spirit realm and dreaming dreams
at young ages are those the Lord has gifted in prophecy, intercession,
and discernment.

The true fact is the enemy has never and will never play fair. He
wants to attack us in order to stop our identity, gifting, and calling
in God's kingdom. Those who are called to see and hear will be

attacked in those areas from a young age in an attempt to bring fear, discouragement, and a crippling halt to the exact gifting the Lord has designed to release.

Your Sons and Daughters Shall Prophesy

One truth I have learned through my children and ministering to the next generation is that there is not a junior Holy Spirit. I have witnessed firsthand children responding to the Holy Spirit and His revelation more freely than adults. Children are sensitive to the spirit realm, and God has used them numerous times in my life and in ministry sessions to speak what is happening spiritually.

We are all familiar with Acts 2:17 (AMP):

> And it shall come to pass in the last days, God declares, that I will pour out My Spirit upon all mankind, and your sons and your daughters shall prophesy [telling forth the divine counsels] and your young men shall see visions (divinely granted appearances).

Amen! This scripture reveals that the great gift God had reserved till the last days is being poured out freely. All are to know the touch of the Spirit of God; both daughters and sons are to be empowered by Him. It is happening now, and it will continue to increase. Reading this book, you are probably thinking through instances when your child or teenager has been the eyes to see, the ears to hear, the dreamer to dream, or the prophet to speak. Moving ahead, let's learn how we can stop the assignments of darkness unleashed to hinder the full release of these gifts.

So What Do We Do?

Maybe you have a child or know a child who has encountered the same experience of nighttime visits as Kendall. Or you might be aware of a child who is afraid at night because of what they see, hear, or experience. Let's look at how to handle these situations.

~ What is in the home?

First, you want to ensure you are not glorifying the enemy in your home. We will examine this further, but for the sake of our discussion now, I will briefly mention a few items. If there are objects of a demonic nature, this will be a red carpet invitation to the harassment the child is experiencing. What type of games does the child play? Are they violent? Is he reading books and playing games about witchcraft or vampires? What type of music, books, movies, and entertainment are present in the home? Are there magazines with sexual overtones? What about pornographic material? Does the child's clothing or jewelry contain demonic symbols? Are there any horror movies? Are there objects of idolatry in the home? These could be items purchased on vacation that depict idols or some sort of false god. The demonic realm can and will attach themselves to inanimate objects in order to gain an entrance into our homes. If the answer is yes to any of these questions, the correct response is to destroy it, repent for allowing these items into your home, and pray, commanding all darkness to go in Jesus's name. The following story clearly illustrates why this is crucial.

Greg and I ministered to nine-year-old Lisa. She was having repeated bad dreams and demonic visitations. In these encounters she would see a snake. When it appeared, it would bite her in the stomach. From the first night she had this dream, Lisa had been suffering chronic stomach pain. Wanting to get her daughter help, the mother had taken her to the doctor, where all exams reported a healthy child. There was no medical explanation for the pain.

As we prayed, I felt the Lord leading me to ask if she had ever received salvation. Even though she regularly attended church, it was apparent she had not yet made this decision and confession. We shared the gospel message, and Lisa was saved. A strong peace came over her. But she soon said, "Miss Becca, my stomach still hurts really bad." We knew then that there was still a deliverance concern that needed to be addressed.

We then began the investigation phase of this session. We asked the mom if Lisa had watched any scary movies. The mother explained that she was not allowed to do this. I inquired if there were horror movies in the home. The mom answered, "Yes, my husband has a bookshelf full of them. He watches them all the time, but Lisa is not allowed to." We explained that it does not matter if she is not allowed to watch them, having the movies in the home was an open door to the demonic harassment. After learning the names of the movies, we prayed and broke the demonic assignment of death and witchcraft off of Lisa. Relieved she exclaimed, "The pain just left. It is gone. My stomach does not hurt anymore!" We rejoiced in her newfound freedom and ended the session with instructions to the mother to repent for allowing these movies into the home, to destroy them, to command all darkness in the home to leave, and to dedicate the home to God and His righteousness. Even the husband was willing to part with the horror movies once he heard the news of Lisa's freedom. He wanted nothing to do with them any longer.

~ Taking action

If a child is having repeated nighttime visitations resulting in fear, it is time to do something about it. When these visitations occur, do not take your fearful child and place her in bed with you. This teaches the child to run from darkness and the resulting fear instead of learning the process of trusting God to deliver her in her time of distress. It is necessary to take action and command the spirit to go in order to restore peace to your child and home.

When the fear comes, ask your child if she is seeing something. If the response is yes, then you want to find out if it is a good or bad visitor. If it is bad, it is time for the evil spirit to leave. When praying, do it in a manner that will not frighten your child. In a calm voice (you do not have to scream; demons are not deaf), you need to command the spirit to leave the child's room. Ask your child if the bad spirit has left. Then ask God to send His angels. Once the child has witnessed this, you want to place her back in bed and welcome the peace of the Lord. Usually, the child is very aware of this peace and will drift back to sleep easily.

If the child shares that what she is seeing is good, use this as a teaching opportunity concerning angels. Explain they are there to protect, to minister, or possibly to relay a message. Now would be a good time to share that the Bible reveals occurrences when grown men fell down in the presence of angels. Even good things when first seen can be intimidating. Again, pray and ask the Lord to release peace.

~ Teaching authority in a healthy manner

After we had that second encounter with demonic activity trying to torment our daughter, the spirit tried to return the following night. At the counsel of our pastor, we were prepared for this. But remember, during the second encounter we had encouraged Kendall to pray with us, releasing her little voice and authority. We did not tell her to shout loudly but to pray out loud with an expectancy of faith that the command would be obeyed. When we model prayer in this manner, it begins to train the child in understanding the authority she walks in and the faithfulness of God to hear and respond. This sets the foundation for how this young one will continue to respond to situations, especially spiritual issues throughout the growing years and into adulthood.

I want to be clear. We did not have our daughter regularly commanding demons. We stood with her when fear was taking advantage of her, and together we took authority. We will discuss this further, but if we focus on darkness too much with our children, then this becomes the open door for the torment in the child's life.

~ Prayers of protection

After Kendall overcame her nighttime visitations, I added a few requests to her bedtime prayers to prevent this demonic spirit from frightening her again. I prayed, "Lord, I thank You for a consuming wall of fire of protection to be around Kendall. I ask that You send Your angels to protect her." One evening I inquired if the angel was there. Smiling, she responded, "Yes!" But this night two-year-old Kendall began to teach me. "Momma, the angel always here now. It not leave me. You have angel too, Momma, and Dadda too." I recall leaving her room knowing this child definitely has a seeing gift.

~ Praying during the night hours

One practice that will greatly benefit children who are tormented at night is to pray over them while they sleep. I advise you to do this as long as the child still needs freedom. Once the freedom comes, it is no longer necessary. When praying, it is important to do it in a whisper. You do not want to wake the child. It is key to know that when we address darkness, it must be done in an audible voice with open eyes. We never close our eyes to darkness because this would show respect where respect is not due. Demons do not have the all-knowing supernatural power to know what we are praying in our mind and spirit. Therefore pray aloud. Below is a sample prayer. We will use the name "Ben" for the sake of example.

> *Father, thank You for little Ben and for Your love for him. Thank You for the precious gift and joy he is. Holy Spirit, I ask that Your presence fill this room. Let Your peace envelop him as he sleeps. We call for an anointing for deliverance to be present and that this night Ben will be set free from the harassing assignments of darkness. In Jesus's name, I command all spirits of darkness, all spirits of fear, death, perversion, rejection* [you want to pray as the Lord leads or as you discern concerning the identity of the spirits] *to get off of Ben now. Loose his dream life. Get out of his thought life and off of his emotions. All assignments in the night hours to establish a stronghold in Ben's life are canceled. You are not welcome here, and I break your power and cut off all evil plots against Ben. Get out of our home. Go now!*

Then release what our heavenly Father has designed for Ben.

> *Father, thank You that everywhere Ben's spiritual house has been swept clean, You come and fill him up to overflowing with Your Spirit and love. Where there has been fear, we speak boldness, courage, and a sound mind. Where there have been scary dreams of death, we speak life and good dreams of Jesus,*

His angels, and Your love. Where there have been perverse dreams and thoughts, we speak purity. Where rejection has tried to steal Ben's identity, we speak the security and love of Jesus into his thought life and emotions. Ben, you are a mighty young man of God and precious in the Lord's sight. You are a son of the King of kings and Lord of lords. Let Your Father's heart of love and acceptance fill Ben now. Lord, send Your angels. I pray a consuming wall of fire of protection to be around Ben and that You seal the work that has been done here by the blood of the Lamb. Thank You, Lord. Amen!

Soon you will begin to see changes in your child. Some might be instant, and some you may notice over a period of time.

What Happened With Previous Owners?

Julie and Ron were overjoyed at the birth of their beautiful daughter Sarah. As all new parents are, they were anxious to bring her home to start their new life together. Julie noticed that Sarah never slept any later than 5:00 a.m. Because Sarah was a newborn, Julie did not feel there was anything to worry about. However, little Sarah would not sleep longer than thirty minutes at a time even during the day. It was exhausting. Around six months, after her nighttime feedings Sarah began to have screaming episodes. Julie still thought it was due to Sarah's young age. As these episodes intensified, Julie knew something was wrong. She was told Sarah was having night terrors. They prayed, and the screaming fits continued. By the time Sarah was two years old, it was obvious that she was in outright fear.

One evening the screams of fear escalated to such a point that Ron took Sarah out of the crib and placed her in bed between him and Julie. Sarah did seem to rest better. Being crowded in the bed, Julie was unable to sleep and decided to sleep in the spare bedroom. She had not slept in this room since they lived in their home. As she drifted back to sleep, Julie had a very disturbing dream. In the dream she walked into a room in which there was a circle of women. The leader of the group approached her and said, "We have been praying against you."

She then tried to choke Julie. She woke up quickly as she began to choke in her sleep. Disturbed, she left the room and went downstairs to her living room.

As they were preparing to go to church the next morning, Julie made her way down the hall. She saw Sarah waiting for her at the top of the stairs. Just like that, before Julie could get to her, she went from standing perfectly still to tumbling down the stairs. It was as if something pushed Sarah forcefully. Thankfully she was not hurt.

Julie decided that it was time to say something to the church prayer leader. She explained everything. They quickly decided that a prayer team needed to pray in their home. As they gathered, the team felt they were to pray in Sarah's room and the spare bedroom. Receiving revelation from the Lord, they perceived that there was some form of abuse that had occurred in those rooms by previous owners. They prayed and commanded all abuse, perversion, violence, and trauma to leave. They announced that all assignments of darkness were broken and invited the Lord's peace and presence into those rooms. Shortly afterward, they learned that while the previous owners lived in that home, the grandparents had sexually abused their grandchildren in those two rooms. From the time the team prayed, Sarah began sleeping through the night until 9:00 a.m. or even later. All screaming episodes totally stopped, and she slept peacefully during naptime. Julie said she quickly realized she had a child who loved to sleep, but it took two years to discover it!

Discerning Within Your Home

This is one topic all believers should be aware of and practice. When we purchase homes, we need to dedicate the land and the property to God. As we learned in the above story, little Sarah was in fear from her time of birth until two years of age from the demonic activity from the previous owners. If there was sin released on the land or in the home, especially repeated sin, the demonic doors will remain open until they are closed. Even under your new ownership, the dark realm will take advantage of this opportunity to terrorize the children.

The opening story I shared concerning our oldest daughter, Kendall, is an example of a demonic visitation to bring fear onto a person. The stories concerning Lisa and Sarah are examples where the demonic had established a habitation in the home. To rid the home of this dark presence will require deliverance. What are the symptoms of a defiled home and land?

+ Sudden chronic illness

+ Recurrent bad dreams and nightmares

+ Insomnia or unusual sleepiness

+ Behavioral problems

+ Relational problems—fighting, bickering, poor communication

+ Lack of peace

+ Disturbed children

+ Unexplained illness or bondage

+ Ghosts or demonic apparitions (especially when the children are visited frequently)

+ The movement of physical objects by the demonic

+ Foul, unexplainable odors

+ Difficulty breathing

+ Continual nausea and headaches

+ Financial difficulties

Praying in Your Home

For those who are saying, "My home is a habitation," it is time to pray. Here are the following steps to take:

1. Repent to the Lord for all defilement that occurred on the land and in the home from the previous owners.

Repentance breaks the back of the enemy as it places all sin under the blood of Jesus.

2. Pray aloud, commanding all spirits of darkness to leave. As you do, remember to pray with your eyes open. We do not want to show respect where it is not due! Here's a sample prayer you can build off of:

Lord, as the homeowners of this house, we want to thank You for the gift You have given us. We are excited about all we are learning about how to protect our home and children. Your Word states in 1 John 4:4, "You are of God, little children, and have overcome them, because He who is in you is greater than he who is in the world" (NKJV). It is from this authority of You living in us that we pray. We say in agreement that all demonic spirits inhabiting this home must go now in Jesus's name. All spirits of death, leave now. All perversion and activities of sexual abuse, we command you to leave our property. [You will want to insert here the spirits that are in operation in your home.] You will no longer harass our family. You have been given your eviction notice. Your assignment here is canceled. We say you will not return to this home or land.

3. Dedicate your home to the Lord.

Lord, we desire holiness as You are holy. We bring our home before You, dedicating it to You and Your purposes. May Your peace, love, and joy fill our dwelling. Where there has been demonic activity, we welcome the activity of Your angels in the walls of this house and the boundaries of this property. And we say, "As for me and our house, we will serve the Lord."

Chapter 3

Whose Demon Is It?

B ILLY IS A cute boy with a witty personality. When he walks into the room, all eyes are drawn to him. He oftentimes will cause the room to break into laughter with his outspoken three-year-old opinions. Sadly, Billy came from a rough background—child sexual abuse, alcohol and drug addictions, and neglect. The foster parents placed over his care learned from the stories Billy shares that somehow his crib was treated like a cage by his birth parents. Therefore, even at the young age of three, the generational issues of rejection, anger, perversion, rebellion, and abandonment from his birth parents and family line were establishing a firm grip. From the trauma of being "caged," these generational issues established strongholds in Billy, making him feel they were his friends.

Thankfully, Billy's Christian foster parents know the importance of deliverance ministry. Seeing his intense struggle with rebellion and anger, they began to pray for him to see him set free. There was one evening when things intensified into a full-blown deliverance session. As they prayed, breaking all soul ties with a spirit of rebellion and generational curses between Billy and his parents, Billy made an interesting statement: "He [meaning the spirit of rebellion] is my friend. He has been with me a long time." The reality is, he was not saying this because he wanted the spirit of rebellion to stay, but he was explaining that he knew the spirit well and it had been with him his entire three-year life. His foster parents immediately broke the power of that lie and commanded the spirit of rebellion to go. Billy responded, "My friend is gone! He is gone!" Since that time, if Billy is asked about his friend, his response is, "My friend is gone, and I am glad he is."

Generational Influences

The truth is, parents will see the need for their child to receive prayer. More times than not, most children, because of their lack of life experiences, are dealing with open doors due to generational influences that have been passed down the family line. Commonly you will hear this referred to as a generational curse or iniquity.

Choices made throughout our lives play a strong role in determining our spiritual condition. Choices we made in our past can continue to have a bearing on the present. But we can look even further. Sinful actions made by our ancestors in previous generations can actually open doors to demonic influences in our lives. The result is commonly referred to as a generational curse or familial spirit—familial meaning ancestral. Until the sinful choices of ancestors are repented of and broken off the family line, future generations will continue to struggle with the same demons. The idea of passing down the effects of sin is found in the second commandment:

> You shall not make for yourself an idol in the form of anything in heaven above or on the earth beneath or in the waters below. You shall not bow down to them to worship them; for I, the LORD your God, am a jealous God, punishing the children for the sin of the fathers to the third and fourth generation of those who hate me, but showing love to a thousand [generations] of those who love me and keep my commandments.
>
> —EXODUS 20:4–6, NIV

Common Generational Curses

Once I became involved in deliverance ministry, I promptly discovered that generational curses are widespread. Virtually any form of demonic oppression can be passed down from one generation to the next. The following are some of the most common types of generational influences. I realize secret societies, other world religions, and pagan practices are included. Our world continues to grow smaller and smaller. All of the issues below are ones that are dealt with in deliverance in this younger generation.

~ Fear and rejection

Frequent, widespread generational curses that are experienced in the younger generation are rejection and fear. If the parent is struggling with these issues, many times one or more of their children will also struggle.

~ Addictions and bondage

When someone battles with an addiction to an abusive substance, more times than not, past family members have suffered the same bondage. It is not strange to hear remarks like this: "I suffer with an addiction to alcohol. My mother was an alcoholic, and her father was also an alcoholic." The enemy will maintain a solid grip on the family line until the issue is repented of, all ties are broken, and the demonic influence is cut off.

~ Sexual abuse and sin

Another recurrent but very sad generational curse that is witnessed regularly in this younger generation is sexual abuse. You often hear stories of one of the parents having been sexually abused as a child, and consequently, around the same age or younger, their child will have been sexually violated. If it is not done by the hands of the parents, then it will be done by another individual close to the child. The enemy does not ever play fair. These spirits of darkness will reinitiate the generational curse until it is broken off the family line. In these situations, not only will the child need deliverance from the generational curse, but also the parent will as well.

~ Freemasonry

I deal with Freemasonry on a consistent basis. Large numbers of men, women, and children have been members or have a family history of participation in this secret society. On the surface, Freemasonry appears as a reputable organization. Membership involves, for instance, generous contributions to charitable organizations, and many important figures have been members. But Freemasonry also has pagan and demonic roots.

Freemasonry has its origins in the worship of Isis, Osiris, and Horus, pagan gods of ancient Egypt. All the tenets of this secret society come from the worship of these demons. The following is a quote from *Morals and Dogmas*, a book written for masons containing lectures of the Ancient and Accepted Scottish Rite, which explain in depth the spiritual origins and beliefs behind the Rituals of Degrees. The author is Albert Pike, the Grand Commander of the Scottish Rite for the Southern Jurisdiction of the United States from 1858–1891. It discusses the Twenty-Fifth Degree, Knight of the Brazen Serpent.

> This Degree is both philosophical and moral. While it teaches the necessity of reformation as well as repentance, as a means of obtaining mercy and forgiveness, it is also devoted to an explanation of the symbols of Masonry; and especially to those which are connected with that ancient and universal legend, of which that of Khir-Om Abi is but a variation; that legend which, representing a murder or a death, and a restoration to life, by a drama in which figure Osiris, Isis and Horus, Atys and Cybele, Adonis and Venus, the Cabiri, Dionusos, and many another representative of the active and passive Powers of Nature, taught the Initiates in the Mysteries that the rule of Evil and Darkness is but temporary, and that of Light and Good will be eternal.[1]

Freemasonry endorses the Luciferian doctrine, which declares that Satan is just as evil as God is good, meaning that the enemy is as powerful as our heavenly Father. All members are free to worship the deity of their choice and are told that the god they worship is the true way to eternal life. It is taught and believed that all Freemasons have a universal god above all other gods, including the Father, Son, and Holy Spirit. Unfortunately, many of these beliefs are not revealed until a member has reached higher levels of leadership.

The list can go on and on concerning the anti-Christian foundation of Freemasonry. After reading this little bit of information, we can see how easy it is for membership in the lodge to release a curse on the member and his family. Young children involved in DeMolay and Job's Daughters are opened to the demonic realm. A spirit of death and infirmity are common spiritual conditions of members. It is not unusual for sudden and premature deaths of active members to occur. A spirit of witchcraft, an anti-Christ spirit, a lying spirit, and a spirit of mammon are very prevalent in those who have actively participated in or have a family connection to Freemasonry. If your family has connections to this organization, a great prayer to pray is the "Prayer of Release for Freemasons and Their Descendents" written by my friend Selwyn Stevens. You can go to www.jubilee.org.nz/prayers/freemasonry and print out the prayer. Parents can pray in agreement that the generational curses are broken, all involvement in this secret society is stopped, and all objects in the home from this organization destroyed.

Hinduism

Hindus practice rites of passage called a *samskara*. They are ceremonies that mark important events in the life of an individual. They generally include ceremonies for prebirth, birth, life, death, and afterlife. In Sanskrit the word *samskara* literally means "making perfect" or "refining," and so a *samskara* is a ceremony that refines or raises an individual beyond his mere physical existence, marking a higher spiritual existence. *Samskaras* bind an individual into his social group.

The ceremonies are performed with the help of a priest and in the presence of family and friends. The most common ceremonies for the young are a prebirth ceremony (*Simantonnayana*), the name-giving ceremony (*Namakarana*), a first-grains ceremony (*Annaprashanna*), the first haircutting (*Mundan*), starting school (*Vidyarambham*), and the thread-giving ceremony (*Upanayana*).

These rituals prove to be a great open door to the Hindu demon gods and goddesses and all the spirits of darkness they represent. This religion is now widespread in our nation. We must be equipped to pray effectively.

Buddhism

In Buddhist baby dedications, newborns are given to Buddha. The parents will speak a vow such as the following:

> *You do not belong to us. You belong to all the Buddhas and bodhisattvas. You belong to all conscious beings in this universe. We will do our best to raise you so that you will be aware of your own Buddha nature—the basic purity of your mind that is your potential to become a fully enlightened being. We will help you to cultivate this aspect of your Buddha nature. We want you to have a self-confidence that is based not on transient, superficial factors but on a deep awareness of your own inner goodness.*

Everyone then chants the mantra of Chenresig (the Buddha of Compassion), visualizing Chenresig above the head of each baby. Light flows from the Buddha of Compassion into the babies, purifying, protecting, and bringing all realizations of the path to enlightenment.

Pagan Baby Dedications

In paganism, children receive a pagan blessing at birth. To introduce the new baby to the extended network of friends and family, a naming ceremony is performed. In some traditions, this is called a "saining," and in others a "Wiccaning." The purpose is the chance to present the baby to the community to which he or she belongs, and to dedicate the child to demon gods and goddesses associated with paganism. It ensures that the baby is a part of something greater, placing the infant under the protection of those present.

A name is chosen before the ceremony. Many choose pagan demonic names that represent darkness and magic. The parents may appoint guardians for their child, a position similar to the Christian concept of godparents. In this ceremony the parents take on the role of high priest and priestess.

The ritual is held outside or in a hall that is consecrated by pagan practices. A table is placed in the center and used as an altar. The guests are invited to form a circle around the altar. If the parents normally call the quarters, it is done now. Calling the quarters is inviting the symbolic energies from the east, west, north, and south to attend, watch over the working, and become part of the magic in the ceremony. The gods of the parents' tradition are called upon and asked to join in the naming of the baby.

1. The baby is placed on the altar. The parent uses the blessing oil to trace a pentagram (or other traditional symbol) on the baby's forehead, saying, "May the gods keep this child pure and perfect, and let anything that is negative stay far beyond her world."

2. A drop of milk is touched to the baby's lips as a blessing of good fortune by the gods that are invoked.

3. The leader then uses the blessing oil to trace the pentagram (or other symbol) upon the baby's chest, saying, "You are known to the gods and to us as [baby's name]. This is your name, and it is powerful. Bear your name with honor, and may the gods bless you on this and every day."

4. The cup of water or wine is passed around the circle. Each guest takes a sip.

5. When the cup reaches the guardians, another blessing to the gods is invoked.

6. Finally, the parents hold the baby up to the sky so the gods can get a good look at the new child. The group is asked to focus on a blessing for the child.

Other More Common Generational Influences

Pride, stubbornness, witchcraft, infirmities, perversion, fear of death, deaf and dumb spirit, depression—are all spiritual issues that are commonly dealt with in young children as generational influences.

The list of demonic strongholds in the appendix will guide you in discovering the spirits in operation. The most important factor is to discover them and to break their hold on the child, ensuring freedom.

Soul Ties

In the story of Billy I referred to the term *soul tie*. Soul ties are emotional and spiritual connections between those who jointly engage in sinful practices. One of the most prevalent ways soul ties are established is through all forms of sexual sin. They are also established in acts of violation and trauma and in relationships based on ungodly control and unhealthy emotional attachment.

One common way soul ties are established between children is through vows made between best friends. These little rituals are normally sealed by the pricking of fingers and the intermingling of blood, signifying the importance of this bond. Sometimes necklaces are exchanged, where one child wears the word *best* and the other child wears the word *friend*. While this might appear to be innocent, if these types of vows and pacts are made, then soul ties have been formed.

Soul ties are easily formed between the generations in a family line if generational curses are not broken and cut off. Once a soul tie is established between two individuals, the demonic can transfer from one person to the other. In other words, if one participant struggles with a rebellious spirit, this demon now has access to the other person. The result is double trouble.

Breaking the Stronghold of
Addictions and Fatherlessness

Cindy's father was a very controlling man gripped by addictions and violence. Even though he served in a city role of protecting the public, he himself was not practicing this in his home. Eventually his bad behaviors and addictions caught up with him. He broke the law, lost his job, and paid for his crimes.

He left home while Cindy was a toddler. She was raised without his negative influence. But when there is a strong, repeated generational pattern that the enemy establishes, even children who are not in the presence of a parent gripped by darkness can experience the same bondage. Satan and his army are legalists and, in their attempt to keep a demonic hold, will continue to attach themselves with their evil agendas until the generational curses and soul ties are broken and under the blood of Jesus.

In her younger years Cindy was drawn like a magnet to drinking and drugs. It was as if a compulsion deep within her drew her to this lifestyle. She was lured into every trap the enemy could set in order to ensure her drug abuse and addiction. We have to understand that the enemy and his army of darkness do not want children to know or understand the love of our heavenly Father. Our foe will perpetuate lies and cause hurtful situations in order to establish his trap of lies.

Following an evening service, Cindy made her way to the altar. You could see the torment in this young girl's life. I quickly made my way to her and began to minister freedom out of the tangible presence of the Father's love. I received prophetic revelation concerning her abusive, absent father and the severe harm this generational curse had unleashed. I knew we had to break the generational curse of bondage to addictions between her and her father. I also knew the Lord wanted to bless her with His father's heart in order to pave the way for her freedom. I asked a man in the church who related to her as a spiritual father to do a healing act. He stood as a male figure in her life and repented to her on behalf of men, her father, and the fatherlessness that had followed her throughout her life. He repented for the violence, neglect, and drug addictions that a man, her father, had allowed. Cindy began to weep as the genuine love of her spiritual and heavenly Father touched her heart. He wept as he began to tell her how beautiful she was and how proud he was of her. "Cindy, you are beautiful. God has amazing things in store for you. I believe in you. These issues with your father no longer have to hold you. Tonight is the night to let this go and receive your freedom."

Cindy truly had desired freedom from the addictions. She would be able to keep herself free for a period of time, but soon she would fall back into the grip of this bondage. Cindy had truly forgiven her father, but this generational curse and the unholy soul tie between her and her father continued to pull her back into the demonic cycle of addiction. After her spiritual father prayed, I began to break the generational curse of bondage, addiction, violence, neglect, and fatherlessness. I severed the unholy soul ties between her and her father and his generations all the way back to Adam and Eve. She received amazing liberty and was transforming before our eyes. Her cheek color went from pale white to rosy pink. Her sadness turned to joy and laughter. Cindy had other issues that needed ministry in the near future to bring her complete breakthrough, but from that night addictive behavior totally left her, and she has not relapsed again.

Out of the Overflow of the Heart the Mouth Speaks

Isn't the delivering power of our God awesome? As I mentioned in chapter 2, unfortunately I have seen repeatedly throughout the years parents who have a preoccupation and fear concerning darkness. I have seen them driven by superstitious fear that the enemy is going to harm their children. As a result, they focus on the enemy and his lies, are overly protective, and even use comments like, "If you do that, it will open you up to attack from the enemy. You better watch out, or the enemy will take advantage of you." I have even heard comments such as the following: "You are such a threat to darkness that witches are cursing you." Or, "Oh my goodness, I forgot to pray protection over you today; we must stop everything and do it now!" These are fear-driven comments and behaviors. These kinds of responses place fear on the child and usually cause resentment toward the parent whose constant focus seems totally targeted in the wrong direction. They may also cause the child to become completely preoccupied and obsessed with darkness. When parents function in this manner, the enemy has room to totally win the battle with their children. We are teaching them that Satan and his minions are more powerful than our God.

I absolutely believe we have to protect our children from harm and things that could be an open door to the demonic. This is the entire reason for this book. But this type of behavior that is completely focused on evil and consistently glorifying the enemy's power might be the exact cause and open door to demonic influence in the life of a child.

What About Discipline?

Sometimes when we are discussing how to keep, guard, and protect our children, the truth concerning righteous discipline is overlooked. I have seen firsthand many parents who are unwilling to discipline their children. In an attempt to be "the best friend" and "the cool parent," clear boundaries and guidelines are not established. Proper boundaries when around other individuals, in someone else's home, or when out in public are not instilled. Instead of showing love and protection through consistency, oftentimes the inappropriate behavior is encouraged through the parents' laughter, which teaches the child the incorrect action is cute and can gain attention. Establishing healthy guidelines and rules for the children from a young age through adolescence will provide a hedge of protection as the child moves through life. When wrong is done, there needs to be reliable consequences as a result. It is important to know the most appropriate and effective form of discipline for each child. Do not be afraid or shy of establishing this fair and healthy environment within the home.

God gives us perimeters in which we are to operate. He is our Father and wants to guide and protect us. Therefore, just as God establishes guidelines, we too are to establish healthy limits with our children and be steady in keeping them.

Now we absolutely need to discipline, but if the discipline is harsh, demeaning, belittling, done in anger, or in an attempt to intimidate or humiliate the child, then this can become an open door for low self-esteem, rejection, a victim spirit, and an orphan spirit. God is the kindest, most loving Father I know. He is never mean or condemning. Even in times of correction or growing into maturity, I never feel condemned. I always feel loved, embraced, and accepted by Him.

Truthfully, most young people determine their view of God based on their experiences with their father and mother. If a father and mother are aloof, distant, or do not take the time to care, then to them this means God is the same way. Or if the father or mother is angry and screams, yells, threatens physical abuse, or goes too far in discipline, then the victim of this treatment becomes just that—a victim throughout their lives. The thought becomes, "Dad is always too harsh and mean, so this has to be how God is." "Mom is depressed all the time or too busy to bother with me. She doesn't care." Or maybe words and actions of affection are not a normal part of interaction in the home. The result is a wounded individual who feels orphaned by his earthly father and mother and also by God.

It becomes very difficult to fathom the true image of our heavenly Father through the skewed fog and haze experienced with the earthly parents. The reality of the attributes of God who is a Father of never-ending, forgiving, accepting, unconditional love; unfailing faithfulness; grace; mercy; hope; all power to protect; surpassing greatness; and so much more is not a clear truth or image to this child. The result: spirits of rejection and abandonment, a victim spirit, and an orphan spirit.

Perfectionism and Unfair Expectations

Sally was ready for a relaxing weekend. She had been through a long week at school with her honors courses and extracurricular activities. But this weekend was going to be fun. All of her grandparents would be coming for a visit. This meant sitting at the table for great meals, fun family conversations, playing games, and watching movies. With her excitement also came dread. Sally wondered if her mother would be able to relax this time. "Maybe Mom will relax and have fun. That would be nice. I really hope she does not expect Jen and me to be the perfect little girls on display this weekend."

Sally and Jen have a great home full of love and encouragement, but their mother, Martha, is driven by perfectionism. Everything has to be picture perfect all the time, especially when family members come to visit. Martha also has a difficult time when there are emotional struggles in the lives of her teenage daughters. She seems to not have the capability to really help them maneuver through these times. Unfortunately, this particular weekend with family proved no different.

Sally and Jen were dressed in their perfect outfits and were expected to sit in the family room all day in order to be in view and on call for whenever their grandparents decided to wake up from naps. Even if Sally and Jen closed their eyes to rest, Martha sat across the room ready to give a stern, corrective stare at the girls. Martha's expectation for the girls communicated, "You are on display. You do not have the privilege to relax like the rest of the family. You will sit and be alert for whenever the grandparents choose to wake up and want to say something to you."

Sally explained she always felt a weight on her to be perfect and that nothing was ever allowed to be wrong. She loves her mother and had forgiven her, but she also had these lingering feelings that she wasn't pretty enough, was inferior to her peers, and could not measure up. As a result, she became driven and performance oriented in order to gain the approval of others. Even in her early college years she majored in what she felt her parents wanted for her, not what she really felt called to. We broke the power of control and all the unfair performance that was weighing Sally down. We broke the power of the lie the enemy was speaking to her that she was not good enough and could ever completely achieve her goals. We broke the intense need she had to receive others' approval, especially the authority figures in her life. We then had Sally write down the godly truths concerning her identity and instructed her to speak them out loud over herself daily.

As she did, the truth of these promises became a part of her identity, and now Sally is a confident, successful young woman living a life on purpose without feeling as if she has to be perfect or please others. The fear of man is no longer entertained in her life.

Modeling the Love of the Father

Some advice I heard several years ago has inspired me to constantly give my best to my children. The advice, surprisingly, came from someone who was not a parent at all, but rather a nun. It was offered by Mother Teresa.... Following her address, a member of the audience stood and asked, "You have done so much to make the world a better place. What can we do?" He clearly wanted to assist in her work.

Mother Teresa smiled and said simply, "Love your children."

The questioner looked perplexed and seemed about to speak again when Mother Teresa raised her hand. "There are other things you can do," she said, "but that is the best. Love your children. Love your children as much as you can. That is the best."

I can't help but believe that her advice, if followed by all parents and all adults in all places at all times, will transform our world in a generation. Just love the children—all the children. Love them as much as you can. That is best.[2]

What a powerful truth; if we love children as much as we can and the best that we can, we can transform our world in a generation. This chapter is not written to place fear or unrealistic burdens on parents to be perfect. We all will make mistakes while raising our children. But let's focus on those things we can do to protect and nurture our young in a positive manner.

+ Spend quality time.

+ Show affection.

+ Say, "I love you."

+ Speak positive words of affirmation.

+ Take the time to genuinely listen to them.

+ Know the things that are happening in their lives.

+ Be consistent with rules and godly discipline.

+ Pray with your children.

+ Teach them to pray.

+ Read the Word of God together.

+ Be humble, admit wrongs, and apologize.

+ Play, laugh, and have fun together.

+ Keep your word, and follow through with commitments.

+ Regularly attend church.

Generational Curses/Soul Ties

The following is a prayer to guide you in breaking the power of generational curses. For the sake of example, I have included bondage and occult practices. But whatever the Lord is revealing as the generational open doors will become the focus of this prayer.

Lord, we have come before You as a family. Where there has been generational curses of bondage, we repent on behalf of ourselves and our ancestors for allowing those patterns to be established. Where there has been family involvement in the occult, including [Freemasonry, Hinduism, Buddhism, shamanism, or witchcraft], we confess this as sin and repent. We break the power of all witchcraft, anti-Christ and lying spirits, and spirits of mammon. We renounce all generational curses attached to these occult practices and ask that all of these issues be now washed over by Your blood. We say that all generational curses are broken off of the lives of our family. We sever generational curses and unholy soul ties that have been in operation between our family and all past family members in the name of Jesus.

Lord, Your Word says, "Listen, listen to me and eat what is good, and your soul will delight in the richest of fare" (Isa. 55:2, NIV). Today we choose to fill our souls with Your goodness and not the things of this world. We as a family choose to walk in Your ways and Your paths so we will find rest for our souls. Where there has been bondage, we speak and release freedom. We are not victims but victors in Christ. Where there has been witchcraft, divination, and anti-Christ spirits,

Soul ties to
fear,
perfectionism,
infirmities
discipline
abuse,
sexual
immorality,
pornography.
unfair
expectations
idolatry of
holidays.

*we speak truth and the freedom of the Holy Spirit to move in
our lives and to fill us up to overflowing.*

Prayer Preparing for a New Way and New Day

As discipline and focusing too much on darkness, perfectionism, and
unfair expectations have been discussed, maybe the Lord has revealed
areas that need to be worked on and improved. Take some time to pray
through this, and make this the day to start fresh and anew. Possibly
you as parents realize that you need freedom from past experiences in
your childhood. Make sure to contact a deliverance ministry to help
you walk in the complete freedom the Lord has designed for you.

Chapter 4

The Lure of Worldly Influences

MICHAEL HAD ALWAYS been an obedient child and was never a problem to his parents, Mark and Lynn. He loved going to church and being involved in the youth programs. However, Mark and Lynn began noticing changes in his personality. That joy seemed to be slowly fading. There was not the usual peaceful contentment in his attitude. No matter what his parents said to him, it irritated Michael. He even began to respond to them in a disrespectful manner. They could feel the calm, spiritual atmosphere of their home slowly changing. Everyone's peace was disturbed. Concerned, Mark and Lynn began to pray and investigate what was possibly the cause of this sudden shift.

One afternoon Michael invited his new friend, Jason, to the house. As Jason entered the home, Lynn began to feel an uneasiness. She prayed, asking the Lord to show her the cause. Michael asked if Jason could come to church with him that night. Knowing this would be good for Jason, Lynn agreed, and soon Jason began to regularly attend the youth events. Still Michael continued to make negative changes, and nothing seemed to be altering in Jason in spite of his attending church.

One day Michael sat a video game on the entry table. Lynn walked over to investigate. To her dismay it was a game totally steeped in witchcraft. She could feel the darkness emanating from it. She quickly asked Michael, "Where did you get this? Games involving witchcraft, death, and violence are not allowed in our home. Honey, I am concerned. You know the rules."

Michael shared that it was Jason's and that he had left it at the house several days earlier. Lynn quizzed Michael on why he had not informed Jason that those games were not permitted in the home.

Michael responded, "Mom, Jason is right about you and Dad. You are too strict and too Christian. He says that I do not need to listen to you and Dad and that there are more fun things to do in the world than following God. Mom, you need to lighten up. What is the big deal? These games are not going to hurt me. I have been playing them all the time at Jason's house."

Lynn had a hard time believing what her son was saying. It was totally out of character for him. It became obvious that this friendship with Jason was not healthy for Michael. Lynn quickly removed the game from their home. She prayed and broke all witchcraft and rebellion that had entered through this game and the rebellious words Jason had spoken to Michael. That night she and Mark prayed, seeking divine wisdom on how to handle this situation.

The next day Lynn invited Michael to a driving lesson. After a few minutes she instructed Michael to pull the car over to the side of the road. She explained to Michael how much she loved him. She shared how proud they were of him and that he truly was a blessing. She then shared the effects his friendship with Jason and the demonic video games were having. "Michael, you have gone from peaceful to irritable, from joy to anger, and from obedient to mocking. Son, do you really enjoy this? Do you feel these games and this friendship are proving healthy for you? We care about Jason and are going to continue to pray that he receives salvation. But in this friendship, you should be setting the standard of joy, love, peace, and obedience. That is not happening. You are allowing Jason to determine and influence your walk. You are embracing rebellion." Michael began to fight back the tears. "I know, Mom, I feel this. It is a battle. I need your help. Please show me what to do."

Relieved at his response, Lynn prayed for her son. She led him into repentance for embracing rebellious attitudes toward his parents and God. The tangible presence of the Lord filled that car. Michael continued to soften as the Lord touched his heart. Leading Michael in a prayer of repentance, Lynn broke all unholy soul ties of rebellion between Michael and Jason and the effects of the witchcraft and violence released from those video games. She finished by asking the

Holy Spirit to fill Michael to overflowing with love and a submissive and tender spirit toward the Lord.

The change in her son was evident. Michael responded, "Mom, this friendship or those games are not healthy for me. I do not handle them well." Lynn shared that Jason could still attend the youth group, but until there was a change in his behavior, that was the only time they could be together. Michael left that prayer time set free and once again a happy, obedient young man.

Be in This World, but Not of It

> Don't become so well-adjusted to your culture that you fit into it without even thinking. Instead, fix your attention on God.
>
> —ROMANS 12:2, THE MESSAGE

Our world is full of evil influences. The world of entertainment is steeped in sexual, violent, and dark overtones. According to Teen Mania, by the time the average child graduates from high school, he will have watched nineteen thousand hours of TV, including about two hundred thousand sexual acts and one million acts of violence.[1] The Internet can be and many times is an open door to pornography and occult groups. Of our young, 58 percent have been involved in objectionable content on the Web.[2] We have to guard what our children are embracing as their forms of entertainment. If ungodly entertainment is welcomed, then a red carpet invitation has been given to the demonic realm in our and our children's lives. The following is a startling statement made by the American Academy of Pediatrics.

> Exposure to media violence through television, movies, music, and video games can contribute to a variety of physical and mental health problems for children and adolescents, including aggressive behavior, nightmares, desensitization to violence, fear, and depression. Listening to explicit music lyrics can effect schoolwork, social

interactions, and produce significant changes in mood and behavior.[3]

I realize the above statements sound strong, and some of you might not agree, but I frequently see young people whose lives have been negatively affected by the world of entertainment. In order for me to explain what we have discovered, let's look at the reality behind the most popular forms of entertainment and worldly influences that trap our children. I do this not for the sake of controversial debate, but for all to understand the importance of where things come from. What is the root or foundational beliefs behind what is being placed in front of us in the form of entertainment? The enemy is a master at counterfeiting and making something evil appear as good and relative to culture. We should be aware of the foundational beginning of all forms of entertainment we and our children engage in.

Supernatural Television Shows

> Your eye is a lamp for your body. A pure eye lets sunshine into your soul. But an evil eye shuts out the light and plunges you into darkness.
> —MATTHEW 6:22–23, NLT

What are your children watching that can shut out the light of truth and plunge them into the beliefs and a curious desire to welcome darkness, witchcraft, and the supernatural? There are shows portraying magic, psychic powers, and vampires as a normal part of life. Some of the most popular shows for our younger children are steeped in Eastern religion and mysticism. *Pokémon*, meaning "pocket monsters," is one of these shows. There are around 150 creatures, each having their own magical power. It was originally created as an electronic toy for Nintendo's Game Boy, but it has since evolved into a popular cartoon show, movies, and video games; it has also created a great frenzy in the exchanging of Pokémon cards. Children are encouraged to carry the cards on them at all times as they give them Pokémon power that will supposedly make them ready for anything. We have ministered to children who have embraced this show, and their struggles have included violence, rage, nightmares, insomnia, allergies, asthma, and other chronic illnesses.

Bakugan is another current animated series that is steeped in Eastern religion and mysticism. *Bakugan* means "exploding sphere" and teaches the power of six worlds, with each having the ability to draw power from the universe, bring enlightenment, tap into mythical power sources, manipulate light and energy, and so on. It teaches the power within and also the important use of magical cards. This too has evolved into games and video games.

Wizards of Waverly Place is a Disney Channel television series that premiered on October 12, 2007. It won "Outstanding Children's Program" at the Sixty-First Primetime Emmy Awards in 2009. A film adaptation won "Outstanding Children's Program" at the Sixty-Second Primetime Emmy Awards. The story line focuses on three wizard siblings with magical abilities competing to win sole custody of the family powers forever. Some toy stores have a section dedicated to this show. You can buy a Wizards of Waverly Place doll along with a book on how to cast spells. Children can log on to the Disney website and play the online games "Magic Curse Reverse" and "Box of Spells."

There are many other shows that children are viewing that involve the occult, talking with the dead, and witchcraft: *That's So Raven, The Ghost Whisperer, Supernatural, 13: Fear Is Real, Vampire Diaries,* and *Medium.* This list can also include reruns of older shows such as *Charmed, Sabrina the Teenage Witch,* and *Buffy the Vampire Slayer.* Are your children watching these shows? If so, it is time to regroup, rethink, and stop.

Sexual Content in Media

In viewing commercials, we see that sexual content is invading the media. According to reports, many teens view television as an important source of information about birth control, contraception, and pregnancy prevention. They feel television programs give guidance about ideas for how to talk to their boyfriend or girlfriend about sexual issues and norms for sexual behavior.

Television's treatment of sexual content in recent years
has grown increasingly frequent and prominent, raising
important societal concerns in an area when decisions about
sexual behavior inevitably involve public health issues. Each
year in the United States, one of every four sexually active
teens is diagnosed with a sexually transmitted disease
(Institute of Medicine, 1997). Approximately 19 million
STD infections are diagnosed annually, with nearly half
of them affecting teens and young adults between 15–24
years of age (Weinstock, Berman, & Cates, 2004).[4]

In addition, the rates of unplanned pregnancies in the United
States, though down slightly since the early 1990s, is still among the
highest of all industrialized countries.[5] This is driven by the fact that
one-third (31 percent) of young women become pregnant at least once
before reaching their twentieth birthday.[6]

One of the most popular television shows that teens view right now
is *The Secret Life of the American Teenager*. This show deals with a
pregnant teenage girl, a boy who is a sex addict, and many other issues
surrounding sexual activity. Another show is *Degrassi*. Fans will know
there has never been a topic too mundane or controversial. Whether
it be friendships and dating, family issues, physical and mental health,
disabilities, sexual orientation, or sexual bias in sports, the show
has covered it all. But now *Degrassi* has introduced a transgendered
student among its cast of characters. Gracie is a girl who says she is a
boy trapped in a female body. Gracie becomes known as Adam Torres.
The show depicts the struggle with her parents and also getting kicked
out of school sports and bullied for her belief that she is a boy. The
sad reality is our youth look to this show for guidance. Our children
should not be permitted to watch these shows. They will shape their
views on sex and their personal relationships and set them against the
purity and righteousness taught by the Word of God.

Popular Movies

Not only has sex invaded the media, but it is also alarming how witchcraft and violence have aggressively done the same. Movies and television shows containing homosexual relationships, explicit sexual content, and abortion are increasing. Many television shows are steeped in witchcraft, psychic powers, and vampirism. To list all of them would take too much space. But what this form of entertainment accomplishes is numbing our young to these demonic lifestyles and teaching them how to allow these deceptions into their everyday life. This produces kids eager to dabble into witchcraft and the occult, therefore welcoming further darkness into their lives each time a more violent and dark movie is released. The lies that are believed sound something like this: "It is just make believe. This is not true. It can't hurt me." I would like to focus on two of the most popular book/ movies series that have accomplished the task of numbing a generation to their lies of darkness, *Harry Potter* and *Twilight*.

~ Harry Potter

Let's begin by looking at two quotes spoken directly by J. K. Rowling, the author of *Harry Potter*.

> But I never, at any point writing any of the books, worried whether children would understand or whether they would find it funny or whether I would frighten them too much, ever, because I wrote the books entirely for myself. I just went where I wanted to go, and hang the consequences, really.[7]

> Mostly I invent spells, but some of them have particular meanings, like "Avada Kedavra." I bet someone out there knows what that means.[8]

Now some of us might be thinking that these statements are not too damaging in and of themselves. And I am not debating if J. K. Rowling is involved in witchcraft. The point to focus on is the worldwide spiritual mentoring these books and movies are bringing to our young.

For instance, let's investigate the meaning of *Avada Kedavra*, which is one of the many curses invoked by the characters. Emitting a jet of green (blue in the sixth film) light and a rushing noise, the curse causes instant death to the victim.

During an audience interview at the Edinburgh Book Festival, Rowling said:

> Does anyone know where *Avada Kedavra* came from? It is an ancient spell in Aramaic, and it is the original of *abracadabra*, which means "let the thing be destroyed." Originally, it was used to cure illness and the "thing" was the illness, but I decided to make it the "thing" as in the person standing in front of me. I take a lot of liberties with things like that. I twist them round and make them mine.[9]

Another source says:

> The Pagan Federation in Britain has reportedly appointed a special youth officer to deal with the flood of inquiries from children who love the Harry Potter books. Children have more trouble distinguishing reality from fantasy than adults; because the Harry Potter books appear so rooted in real life, many may believe that the magic in the books is real and will therefore explore witchcraft, Wicca, and paganism.[10]

The Word of God says we have the power to bless or curse in the words we speak. Basically, entertainment that is steeped in witchcraft or even its ideology teaches this exact principle. However, the emphasis placed on cursing is from a standpoint of witchcraft, human control, and manipulation; it teaches the young that it is acceptable and helps them gain higher status with their peers. It clearly expresses the belief that personal power, witchcraft, riding brooms, casting spells, self-transformation, and shape-shifting are all something to be desired and obtained. In this series, magic appears as something ordinary.

Harry Potter and the Half-Blood Prince sold nine million copies in the first twenty-four hours of its release.[11] *Harry Potter and the Deathly Hallows* sold 11 million copies in the first twenty-four hours.[12] The books turned into successful movies, all of which have been highly successful in their own right, with the first, *Harry Potter and the Philosopher's Stone*, ranking number eight on the all-time highest grossing films list and three others ranking in the top fifteen. All six films released, so far, placed in the top thirty.[13] The films have birthed eight video games and have led to the licensing of more than four hundred additional Harry Potter products (including an iPod) that have, as of 2005, made the Harry Potter brand worth four billion dollars and J. K. Rowling worth one billion dollars, making her, by some reports, richer than Queen Elizabeth II.[14]

There was a time when those who played with occult games and embraced this kind of entertainment were considered deviant. But these books and movies have now become entry-level occult tools introducing its audience into spiritual power apart from God.

~ Twilight

Upon researching this book series and the movies, I have been stunned to the point of being absolutely speechless at what I have learned. Am I surprised that someone is writing this type of material? Unfortunately, in our fallen world, the answer is no. But I am greatly puzzled at the number of Christians who embrace this series and attempt to liken it to Christianity and our risen Lord, Jesus. I personally find this a far stretch and offensive. But sadly I have spoken with many believers who feel this way. How can Jesus, the Lord of the universe, the unblemished lamb, the Holy One without sin, perfect in love, be compared to a vampire? An evil demonic force who drinks blood (and it does not matter that it is not human blood), a soul damned to hell living in the depths of darkness does not even come close to any sort of resemblance to the beauty of Jesus. He shed His own blood so all men have available to them eternal salvation. He did not take or drink blood from anyone to gain His life and power. He gave His life to give life to all.

Just to give a brief synopsis, Edward and his "coven" of vampire family are vowed good and basically "vegetarian" vampires. They only feed on animal blood. The problem is that Edward wants to eat Bella, his beloved girlfriend, every time the sexual tension escalates. He avoids having sex with her, not because of any moral grounds, but out of fear that he will eat her and cause her to become the "un-dead." Bella loves him and is willing to step into his dark "eternity" no matter the cost. They eventually marry, and in the fourth movie she almost dies giving birth to their half-vampire/half-human child. In order to save her, Edward does an emergency c-section with his own teeth and then injects his venom into her heart and all over her body to turn her into a vampire before she dies.

Stephenie Meyer received a dream on June 2, 2003. The visions she had of a vampire and mortal as lovers compelled her to start writing the story immediately. In summary, Meyer says:

> I woke up (on that June 2nd) from a very vivid dream. In my dream, two people were having an intense conversation in a meadow in the woods. One of these people was just your average girl. The other person was fantastically beautiful, sparkly, and a vampire. They were discussing the difficulties inherent in the facts that A) they were falling in love with each other while B) the vampire was particularly attracted to the scent of her blood, and was having a difficult time restraining himself from killing her immediately.[15]

Meyer states the following concerning the apple on the book cover for *Twilight*.

> The apple on the cover of *Twilight* represents "forbidden fruit." I used the scripture from Genesis (located just after the table of contents) because I loved the phrase "the fruit of the knowledge of good and evil." Isn't this exactly what

Bella ends up with? A working knowledge of what good is, and what evil is. The nice thing about the apple is it has so many symbolic roots. You've got the apple in Snow White, one bite and you're frozen forever in a state of not-quite-death.... Then you have Paris and the golden apple in Greek mythology—look how much trouble *that* started. Apples are quite the versatile fruit. In the end, I love the beautiful simplicity of the picture. To me it says: *choice*.[16]

Meyer also goes on to say that some of the inspiration of the story came from the musical group Marjorie Fair. "For New Moon, they were absolutely essential. They can put you into a suicidal state faster than anything I know.... Their songs really made it beautiful for me."[17] Also as an inspiration for one of her characters was a band called My Chemical Romance. She states, "It's someone...who just wants to go out and blow things up."[18]

Her deception is having quite an impact. The book became an instant best seller when published in hardback in 2005, debuting at number five on the *New York Times* best-seller list within a month of its release and later peaking at number one. That same year *Twilight* was named one of *Publisher's Weekly* best children's books of 2005. The novel was also the biggest selling book of 2008 and, to date, has sold seventeen million copies worldwide, spent over ninety-one weeks on the *New York Times* best-seller list, and been translated into thirty-seven different languages.[19]

On November 20, 2008, fans waited in long lines to see the midnight release of the newest film. This is the report that Fandango gave: "New film overtakes Harry Potter movies as third biggest advance ticket-seller in company history."[20]

The movie carries a spirit of seduction that draws people into its enticing darkness. In a *Rolling Stone* interview, Robert Pattinson, the actor who plays "Edward," was asked, "Is it weird to have girls that are so young have this incredibly sexualized thing around you?" He answered, "It's weird that you get 8-year-old girls coming up to you saying, 'Can you just bite me? I want you to bite me.' It is really strange how young the girls are, considering the book is based on the virtues of chastity, but I think it has the opposite effect on its readers though. [*Laughs*]"21

Meyer shares that she had an encounter with Edward in a dream after *Twilight* was completed. He spoke to her and said that she had gotten it all wrong because he did drink human blood and could not live on only animal blood as she wrote in the story. She says, "We had this conversation, and he was terrifying."22

The reality is, when these dark stories are allowed into our lives, they can establish demonic strongholds. Death, fear, seduction, witchcraft, and anti-Christ spirits are the influences driving these stories. For the sake of an alluring story line written by a Mormon mother, we cannot be gullible. This movie is not just some innocent fantasy. There is a vampire movement that has been gaining momentum since 1977, and there are actual vampire cults where members file their teeth and bite each other until they draw blood, which they then drink. I do not enjoy writing about this material. It is unpleasant. The truth is much of the church is unaware of this danger that is facing this younger generation. Do not read these books or watch these movies. This is what the Word of God has to say in Leviticus 7:26–27 (NKJV):

> Moreover, you shall not eat any blood in any of your dwellings, whether of bird or beast. Whoever eats any blood, that person shall be cut off from his people.

Pagan Beliefs

Cindy Jacobs shares a tactic of the enemy in her book *Deliver Us From Evil*: "There is a plot afoot, and it is a serious threat to the nations of the earth. This plot involves a sugarcoating and mainstreaming of witchcraft. It particularly grips our youth. Satan has done his work well, while most of us as Christians have been asleep. What is his purpose? He seeks to reintroduce and reestablish the worship of ancient gods and goddesses. This is not simply an American phenomenon. From Scandinavia to Germany to Latin America witchcraft is taking root.

Many times it is propagated under the guise of getting back to our roots."[23]

According to the Barna Group, "Three out of every four teenagers have engaged in at least one type of psychic or witchcraft-related activity. Among the most common of those endeavors are using a Ouija board, reading books about witchcraft or Wicca, playing games involving sorcery or witchcraft, having a 'professional' do a palm reading, or having their fortune told. Conversely, during the past year fewer than three out of every ten churched teenagers had received any teaching from their church about elements of the supernatural."[24]

> Seven million teens have encountered an angel, demon, or some other supernatural being. More than two million teens say they have communicated with a dead person (10%). Nearly two million youth claim they have psychic powers.[25]

Wicca

Recently I came face-to-face with the blatant intent of paganism as I took our daughter on the tour of her chosen college campus. As we walked through the student center, there were many tables and resources on display. Making our way to the exit, we noticed the last table was being manned by a young woman dressed in black, with black painted fingernails, black lipstick, and white makeup. The banner draped above the table read, "WICCA—pagan religion." We watched as she spoke with those interested in finding out more about this occult group. The whole scene was ironic. Ten minutes beforehand, I had been approached by a young girl sharing the gospel. She was involved in Campus Crusade for Christ, and that day her job was to interview visitors on campus and in the process share the message of salvation. What a profound difference a few minutes made in our visit. In the entrance, a student sharing the gospel; in the exit, Wiccans spreading their deception.

I am not against those who embrace Wicca and witchcraft; it is my prayer they are saved and set free. It is obvious that they are on a spiritual search for truth, but they are looking in the wrong places. What I am against is what the Word of God tells us to be against: witchcraft and the worship of gods, goddesses, and idolatry. This is exactly what Wicca teaches. Wiccans believe in the worship of a female and male god, the lady and the lord. The lady was created first, so when she needed a companion, the spirit created for her a half-man/half-animal creature called the lord. They believe that Satan is a myth and slander of the true god of light, Lucifer. The lady is usually worshiped in the form of the goddess Lilith, Kali, Tanit, Isis, Astarte, or Diana. They are devout believers in reincarnation and do not believe in heaven or hell but Summerland. From there you are reborn to learn the lessons you need from life. Casting of spells makes up their religious practices. They give the disclaimer of being good witches; therefore they participate in casting good spells and not bad spells. Sexual relationships bring Wiccans into higher spiritual enlightenment and are very often a part of rituals. They have purposefully placed themselves on college campuses in order to snare the youth of our nation into their beliefs.

Children who have embraced this or some other form of paganism will become distant, isolated, and begin wearing dark clothes, black lipstick, and black nail polish. They might even have jewelry with witchcraft symbolism. Books concerning witchcraft might be hidden in their bedrooms. Parents, if you have a child involved in this, all activity with this group and friends associated with it should be stopped. If your child is willing, schedule a session with an experienced deliverance ministry.

Tattoos and Piercings

Tattooing is another fad that is sweeping the nations. It has been around for thousands of years, originating in Egypt and highly practiced by the women of that culture. It was originally used as a marking of a permanent amulet, which was a small object worn to ward off evil or illness. It was believed to bring good fortune. It was also used as a mark for those who were prostitutes or high priestesses in cults. As the use of tattoos evolved into other cultures, it became a mark of religious practices and also the god or goddess that the individual was pledging allegiance to.

As stated earlier, we have to know the foundational beliefs of things we are allowing into our lives. Tattoos have become such an accepted part of our culture that Mattel has released a new Barbie doll called Totally Stylin' Tattoos Barbie. She can even receive a tattoo on the lower part of her back. These are known as tramp stamps. This is a sign worn by girls to relay the message to boys they are "easy" for lack of a better term. Even our young girls are being desensitized and taught that marking their bodies to send sexual messages is appropriate.

Now tattooing and body piercing have evolved into a new fad that is slowly gaining ground called suspension or flying. This practice involves the suspending of bodies through hooks used to pierce the flesh in order to create pain, draw blood, release endorphins, and bring those participating into a place of higher spiritual enlightenment. Some involved in this practice hang suspended by the hooks for extended periods of time. Others will insert the enormous hooks into the skin of their back, be lifted into the air, and literally swing back and forth while suspended in midair. This release of endorphins creates a sense of pleasure in the deep flesh piercings. For those who do this, they are willing to pay the painful price of these hooks and suspend their bodies in order to experience the high and the pleasure of the endorphins. This is a quote from Chris with firebloodbodyart.com.

> We adorn our bodies with generic style paint...somewhat similar to the Aborigines. We are covering our bodies doing the whole tribal thing to give the feel of tribal ordinance to show these do have ceremonial and ritualistic purposes.[26]

> We are doing the whole tribal thing to get people into researching the origins of suspension. Suspension has been done all over the world for thousands of years. Most people don't realize that. I personally use suspension as a release of hormones. Personal therapy even, to try to center myself to ground everything that is going on around me.

When you suspend, although it seems tormenting and it
may hurt a whole lot, it really centers me and allows me to
focus on problems at hand. It will help clear issues up that
are going through your mind.[27]

...Because there is no regulation here, we would like to
start a revolution and maybe get a following of people who
would stand for what piercing needs to be.[28]

Stephen was a godly young man walking with God. But he had
always wanted a tattoo. His reasoning was, "Everyone is doing it. It
will look cool." He had one placed on his right shoulder and soon
began to struggle with oppression. One evening as his future in-laws,
Bill and Susan, were talking with him about how to overcome his
spiritual battle, Stephen suddenly went from sitting calmly in his chair
to being thrown to the floor crying out in great pain. Grabbing his
right shoulder, he cried out, "My shoulder!" Quickly Bill and Susan
broke all witchcraft and death attached to Stephen through that
tattoo. The peace of God flooded over him as freedom was ministered.
He later told Bill and Susan that it felt as if a knife was being thrust
into shoulder until they canceled the demonic power.

Video Games

Video games modeling witchcraft and many times extreme violence
are sweeping through the world with great popularity. Some of the
ones to avoid for children would include Fable, Starcraft, World of
Warcraft, Dungeons and Dragons, Pokémon, Magic 8 Ball, Magic:
The Gathering, Vampire: The Masquerade, Sword and Sorcery,
Masters of the Universe, Snake Mountain, Alien Blood and Monster
Flesh, Beyblade, Legend of Nara, Bakugan, Vampire Diaries, and
Ouija Board. This is not an exhaustive list, but it gives strong direction
of the types of games to keep away from.

According to recent research, it is clear that teens (as well as
adults) are spending more time immersed in video game worlds. These
virtual worlds of fantasy can challenge our minds to be creative, solve

problems, and learn lessons. However, many games such as Quake, Half-Life, System Shock, Manhunt, Resident Evil 5, Dead Rising, Resident Evil 4, Grand Theft Auto, God of War II, Mortal Kombat: Deception, MadWorld, Gears of War, and Saints Row 2 perpetuate evil, sexual darkness, racism, and extreme violence.

Recent studies found that playing violent video games is a way to rehearse violent behaviors, making it easier to bring that behavior into real life. If you practice shooting basketballs thousands of times, you get better at scoring. If you practice killing thousands of times, you get better at that as well. The Columbine shooters, Eric Harris and Dylan Klebold, had been playing "first-person shooters" for more than a year before that fateful day. When the time came to play the game in the real world, they were ready.

Two studies published in the *Journal of Personality and Social Psychology* on April 23, 2000, show eye-opening results. The article clearly demonstrates that violent video games do negatively affect the behavior of the players.

+ The player develops positive attitudes toward the use of violence.

+ The player develops expectations that others will behave aggressively.

+ The player assumes that others have similar attitudes of aggression.

+ The player comes to believe that violent solutions are effective and appropriate for solving problems.

+ The player develops a total disregard for societal norms, property rights, and even the general value of other lives.

+ The player sees the world as a violent, unsafe place (everyone is out to get you).

✦ The player learns that aggressive actions against others,
   such as fighting and shooting, may be appropriate,
   even necessary.

✦ Violent video games have an addictive nature.

✦ Playing can make an already aggressive person even
   more aggressive.

✦ The player becomes more aggressive, changes his out-
   look on life and socializing, and tends to socialize
   with others who demonstrate similar attitudes of
   aggression.

✦ The player's socialization with teachers, parents, and
   nonaggressive peers are likely to degenerate.[29]

Music

The music industry is filled with sinful and inappropriate lyrics and
sounds. Artists such as Jay-Z, Lady Gaga, Eminem, and numerous
others are having a great impact on our youth.

Music, lyrics, and sound can form cultures, subcultures, and
revolutions. There is a deep impact that music has on our emotions,
thought patterns, and beliefs as the words and sounds are repeatedly
sung and listened to. Studies have shown that listening to explicit
music lyrics can affect schoolwork, affect social interactions, and
produce significant changes in mood and behavior.

> On average, American youth listen to music from 1.5 to
> 2.5 hours per day, and an analysis of at-risk youth revealed
> they listen up to 6.8 hours per day. Studies have shown
> that a preference for certain types of music or music videos
> with explicit references to drugs, sex or violence can be
> associated with negative effects on schoolwork, behavior
> and emotions. Heavy metal and hard rock music have also
> been associated with increased suicidal risk, depression
> and delinquent behavior.[30]

For example, a survey of nearly 3000 14- to 16-year-olds found that white boys who engaged in five or more risk-taking behaviors (eg., smoking cigarettes, drinking alcohol, cheating in school, having sex, cutting school, stealing money, smoking marijuana) were most likely to name a heavy metal group as their favorite. The relative risk for engaging in risky behaviors and choosing heavy metal music as a favorite was 2.1 for girls and 1.6 for boys. Similarly, heavy metal music seems to be the preference of teenagers in psychiatric units, especially if they have a conduct disorder.[31]

Another sobering fact that cannot be ignored is the power of the sound of music. In one study, scientists decided to compare the effects of violent heavy metal music with Christian heavy metal music. The results are shocking.

Groups of undergraduate males heard either sexually violent heavy metal rock, Christian heavy metal rock, or easy listening classical music. A month before and immediately after listening, the students answered a questionnaire measuring gender-role stereotyping, adversarial sexual beliefs, acceptance of interpersonal violence, rape myth acceptance (the idea that women invite and/or enjoy rape), and self-reported sexual arousal. The somewhat surprising result was that it did not matter whether participants heard sexually violent heavy metal or Christian heavy metal. Exposure to either type of music produced more negative attitudes toward women. In other words, the lyrics did not make a difference, but the heavy metal musical form did. While there is reason to wonder whether the students really "heard" the lyrics, the larger issue may be that the sound of the music carries a great deal of information independent of lyrical content. "'Angry-sounding' music may increase aggressive thoughts and feelings, regardless of the specific lyrical content."[32]

Parents, we have to be involved in discussions and know and guard the forms of music our children are listening to.

Physical Fitness

I am aware that discussing this is going to disturb some parents and their children. Before further explanation, I want to say I am not against self-defense. It is an important tool to receive training in. And I am not against physical exercise. However, I disagree with practices whose roots are steeped in evil and paganism.

~ Martial arts

I believe that forms of martial arts whose roots are attached to Eastern religions such as Buddhism and Taoism should not be participated in. The religious significance of these fighting sports lies in the harmonizing of life forces (yin and yang) and the ability to harness "ch'i," or universal energy. Yin is the female principle of the universal being known as the moon goddess. Yang is the male principle of the universal deity known as the sun god. Masters in the martial arts are able to accomplish tremendous physical feats. The ability to strike or smash a pile of bricks with a single blow is attributed to ch'i. This is nothing more than a form of humanism and witchcraft manipulation.

Aikido literally translates as the road to a union with the universal spirit. Kung Fu, the original form of all martial arts that dates back to 2696 B.C., is an occultic form of divination called I Ching. I Ching is a system birthed in China predicting the future and giving guidance through the practice of divination. Ninjitsu is a Japanese martial art form that was banned by the emperors in the 1600s because of its occultic powers. Practitioners called Ninjas, are mercenary agents hired for covert operations involving espionage, sabotage, and assassination. They employ mind control, hypnosis, yoga, occult rituals, and other New Age practices.[33] Those who have lined up with this practice will need to repent and break all ties with witchcraft, divination, and the universal ch'i.

John was an athletic young man who enjoyed his weekly workouts in martial arts. Despite his strong physical condition, he began to be plagued with chronic pain in his feet. He could barely walk. It was a rare disorder in which there was no treatment except for a procedure that would temporarily block the pain of the nerve endings. As we ministered to John and broke the power of the demonic and violence connected with his involvement in the martial arts, his feet began to heal, and he is now free from any physical condition and pain.

~ Yoga

This industry brings in over twenty-seven billion dollars in to the United States a year.[34] It is more prosperous than pornography. The word and concept of yoga comes out of Hinduism and means "the path followed so as to realize the god within." It involves the use of special postures and positions along with meditation to produce an altered state of consciousness and ultimately to achieve union with god. All forms of yoga involve an occult philosophical base and assumptions, even that which is presented as a purely physical exercise. Although the beginning level appears only as a form of exercise or gymnastics, breathing, and relaxation exercises, the advanced levels are connected with a mastery of cosmic forces—the practice of spiritistic and magical phenomena.

Shiva is the Hindu god known as the destroyer. While many Hindu deities are associated with the different paths of yoga and mediation, in Shiva, the art of meditation takes its most absolute form. It is believed that the path of Lord Shiva is the path of the ascetic yogi.

Kundalini yoga teaches that seven centers of psychic energy in the body store energy from the universal life force. Various exercises and meditations awaken these centers, allowing the power to rise up the spine, an event called Kundalini. This power can be manipulated to promote healing. The ultimate result is enlightenment.

Why is this embraced and taught inside the walls of the church? Why is it allowed in our schools? In our lack of gaining knowledge, a form of demonic worship has taken root—even to the point where Christian institutions and individual believers unknowingly have become instructors in the ancient worship to Hindu deities.

Lynn was experiencing constant pain in the abdomen area. She was highly involved in yoga and was insistent that this was helping her even though she was living in pain. I shared with her the above history of yoga and the open doors to the demonic she was allowing into her life. Lynn was skeptical to receive what I was sharing. It was explained that if she continued her yoga exercise classes, our prayers could not help her. If we broke the power of witchcraft, Kundalini, and anti-Christ spirits attached to this structure, and she willingly engaged in this activity again, the demonic would came back seven times worse. The team and I continued to speak truth to her. The skepticism soon left, and she was ready to receive prayer.

We first had Lynn repent for opening herself up to a form of exercise rooted in demonic worship. All witchcraft, divination, death, Kundalini, and anti-Christ spirits attached to the worship positions of yoga to the Hindu god of Shiva were broken. Lynn renounced aloud the activity of these spirits in her life. In closing we welcomed the anointing of the Holy Spirit to fill her. Why? Because where the house has been swept clean, we need to fill it with the Spirit of God. The anointing of the Lord moved beautifully, and since that ministry time Lynn has been pain free.

Is There Anything That Is OK?

There are many more topics I could discuss, but I believe we have given a good overview of some of the most popular entertainment and worldly influence fads that are gripping our youth. Five years from now there will be new books, music, music groups, games, video games, computer games, movies, and witchcraft practices that will be alive and well on the scene. I am keenly aware that when I teach on these topics, people become uncomfortable and disturbed. Some do because it is not pleasant discussion; others are uncomfortable because of their involvement in these activities.

The point that we as believers need to grasp is discovering the foundational beliefs behind all that we are embracing. If the roots of the behavior are pagan and demonic or in question, then it is not something we should willingly embrace. If the beginnings are not demonic in nature, then go for it. Yes, movies, books, music, games, and the like can be wonderful. Self-defense is great when it is not done under the structure of martial arts that stem back to Buddhism and Taoism. Stretching and exercise are fine, just not under the system of yoga. I often challenge those involved, "Why not start a self-defense class or stretching exercise program that is not lined up under the names or beliefs of these ancient pagan rituals?" Before we allow our children to step into something, investigate it. What is the original purpose of the practice? Will my child's involvement be an open door to the demonic, or will it be a blessing? What are the lyrics to the songs my children are listening to? What are the beliefs and agendas behind the groups they are listening to? What shows, movies, and cartoons are they watching? What books are they reading? Are they designed to draw children into occult, witchcraft, and violent beliefs? Are the computer games your child plays filled with sexual overtones, violence, and death? If so, why not purchase games such as Civilization Revolution or Wii games that do not teach yoga? Watch out for entertainment that promotes psychic powers, homosexuality, racism, and premarital sex.

What Can the Church Do?

Our young apply equal handling to the supernatural world as they do other forms of expression in their lives. They cut and paste supernatural experiences and views from a mixture of sources—movies and books, personal experiences, the Internet, peers and family members, and any other place they are comfortable with. Most importantly, they are prompted by their desire to discover what works and feels right for them.

The church should be educating their young on the supernatural realm and playing a key role in forming their beliefs. Research reveals that many churches fail to address the subject of the supernatural with sufficient frequency or relevance. It was reported that "only one-quarter of churched teenagers (28 percent) recall receiving any teaching at their church in the last year that helped to shape their views on the supernatural world."[35] David Kinnaman shares in a Barna report:

> This generation is longing for personal meaning and they are comfortable with incredible technological and media-driven tools that would enable them to accomplish

whatever spiritual goals they choose. But millions of teens are precariously close to simply shelving the Christian faith as irrelevant, uninspiring, and "just a phase." Millions of previously churched Busters ended up rejecting Christian spirituality after high school. [This generation is] in even greater danger of making that leap from faith to doubt.

The supernatural world represents the epicenter of the spiritual struggle for their hearts and minds....When teenagers settle for cheap alternatives instead of choosing intimacy with God—and relying upon His care and His power—it can lead to years, even decades, of spiritual entrapment in their lives. But with appropriate choices come spiritual rewards. After Jesus rejected Satan's temptations, His ministry flourished. If our young reject spiritual deception and stop tinkering with contemptible imitations of God's power, it could spell the difference between a generation fulfilling its spiritual destiny and one that turns from God during adulthood.[36]

Ridding Your Homes

After such a heavy chapter, some of you might be wondering how to handle all of this information. If these forms of entertainment or influences are embraced in the home, what do you do?

1. It is time to repent.

2. Break off all power that this entertainment has unleashed onto your child and in your home. The closing prayer will guide you in how to do this.

3. Spiritually clean house. Get rid of all the music, movies, books, comic books, video games, and all objects and possessions that focus on paganism and evil.

4. Choose to stop all involvement in ungodly entertainment and worldly influences, pagan activities, and demonic forms of self-defense and exercise.

5. Do not welcome or allow any of these activities back into your home or the life of your children.

6. Invite the presence of the Lord into your home. Let the supernatural experiences of God, His love, the Word, and His presence shape and mold your children.

Let's Pray

Father, thank You for the truth that is being revealed. It is our heart's desire to walk purely and upright before You. We do not want there to be any open doors over our children or ourselves personally drawing us into darkness. We confess that we have allowed open doors in our home, family, and children to the demonic realm by the forms of entertainment and worldly influences we have entertained. Forgive us for our involvement with [name the movie, book, music, games, exercise techniques, pagan activities, etc. that needs to be repented of].

We now renounce and break all powers of perversion, seduction, witchcraft, divination, fear, fear of death, death, violence, rage, anti-Christ spirits, the practicing of speaking curses, and all enticement to darkness, including werewolves and vampires, Kundalini spirits, and all other spirits of darkness. We command you out of our lives, [child's name] *life, and our home. Go now!*

Father, cleanse our lives and our homes, and fill us with Your love, peace, joy, comfort, submissive spirits to You, and increased discernment. Cause us to walk circumspectly and wisely in all of our activities.

And we make the commitment together aloud and in agreement with Joshua 24:15: "As for me and my house, we will serve the LORD" (NKJV).

Chapter 5

The Truth Behind Peer Pressure

I RECENTLY SAT AROUND a table with fifteen young Christian women from the ages of fifteen to twenty-three. I asked them what they struggled with the most in their daily lives. All of them responded unanimously: "Peer pressure." Now the girls who were homeschooled seem to have less amount of stress in this area, but the other girls who were regularly in school and around other teenagers shared that this was a consistent issue. My heart broke for one particular girl.

Prophetically the Lord revealed that she was having a very difficult time with her peers. She was being left out and made fun of because she had refused to budge in her Christian beliefs and would not engage in sinful actions. I saw a picture of her sitting at the school cafeteria table alone, while other teenagers sat laughing a few feet away. I could see and feel her intense grief. Tears streamed down her face and mine as we both asked God to send her a special best friend to the school. This encounter caused me to further come to terms with the pressure our young live in.

Pressure is defined as "harassment; oppression, a constraining or compelling force or influence; to force (someone) toward a particular end; influence."[1] Peer pressure is defined as "social pressure by members of one's peer group to take certain action, adopt certain values, or otherwise conform to be accepted."[2] Beginning in junior high, groups provide teenagers with identity. Many times future friendships and treatment by fellow peers depend on which cliques a young person hangs out with.

As a mother of three teenage daughters, I am aware of the negativity, darkness, and evil that attempt to influence children. Drugs, alcohol, sex, sexting, cutting, huffing, cheating, lack of respect, suicidal thoughts, and ungodly mind-sets are forces that our children regularly contend with. It seems with each passing generation that the negative influences and pressure increase.

Statistics show that this is a generation with almost no morality or gauge to live by. The following are the latest numbers as shared on Teen Mania's website:[3]

+ One in ten high school females has reported being raped at some point in her life.

+ Fear of violence in schools is now the leading "worry" of public school teens.

+ Of high school seniors, 48 percent are sexually active (had sexual intercourse in the past three months).

School and community gang activity are also on a clear upward trend in many communities across the nation.[4]

Interviews

In my research I came across the following interviews done by the University of Michigan concerning adolescents and peer pressure. I found this to be eye-opening, as I believe you will.

~ Seven-year-old:

Do you know what peer pressure is? *No.*

Have you ever done something, or felt like you had to do something, because one of your friends has done it or because they asked you to do it? *Yes.*

That's peer pressure. Do you remember any of the things you have done because of your friends? *No.*

Do your friends ask you to do things that are wrong and you would get in trouble for? *No.*

Do your friends help you to do better in school? *No.*

If one of your friends does good in school, do you feel like you have to do good too? *Yes.*

Why? *I don't want them to think I am dumb.*

Have you ever tried to make your friends do something you wanted them to do? *No.*

~ Twelve-year-old:

Do you know what peer pressure is? *Yes.*

What does it mean? *It is when your friends try to make you do things.*

Do your friends try to make you do things? *Yes.*

What type of things? (laughter) *They have asked me to throw toilet paper at someone's house on Halloween.*

Have they ever asked you to do more serious things like smoke? *Yes.*

Have they ever asked you to do something and you tell them no? *Yes.*

How did you feel when you told them no? *I feel like they will never speak to me again.*

Then why did you say no? *Because I knew it was the wrong thing to do.*

Have your friends ever talked to you about doing good in school? *No.*

If your friends are doing good in school, do you feel like you have to do good in school too? *Yes.*

Why? *So they won't talk about me and call me names.*

Have your parents ever talked to you about peer pressure? *Yes.*

What did they say? *My mother told me not to let someone make me do something that I don't want to do, use my own mind. She told me to be a leader and not a follower.*

Have you tried to pressure any of your friends into doing anything? *No.*

~ Sixteen-year-old:

Do you know what peer pressure is? *Yes.*

Do you ever feel peer pressure from your friends? *All the time.*

What do you feel pressured to do? *Everything.*

Like what? *Skip school, have sex.*

Do you feel more pressure from your female friends to have sex with guys or from guys to have sex with them? *I feel more pressure from my female friends. They always ask me why I haven't had sex yet.*

What do you tell them? *I tell them I am waiting for the right person.*
Do you ever feel like they wouldn't be your friend if you didn't do what they said? *Not really.*
Do your friends challenge you to do good in school? *No.*
Do you feel like you have to do good in school if they do? *I feel like I have to do good in school, but not because they do.*
Have you ever tried to pressure one of your friends into doing anything? *Something wrong?*
No not necessarily, just anything? *Well, I guess I have.*
Like what? *I don't know. Little things, things that I want them to do for me.*[5]

Negative Peer Pressure

The need for acceptance, approval, and belonging is vital to teens. Teens who feel isolated or rejected by their peers or in their family are more likely to engage in risky behaviors in order to fit in with a group. In this situation, peer pressure can impair good judgment and fuel risk-taking behavior. For example, teens with learning differences or disabilities are often rejected due to their age-inappropriate behavior and are therefore more likely to associate with other rejected or delinquent peers.

Sam, a handsome fifteen-year-old, struggled with a form of high-functioning autism. Due to his condition, he was always made fun of, and even in church youth groups the kids distanced themselves from him. Actually, his ailment was not very noticeable unless you engaged in a lengthy conversation with him. Even then for the most part he was able to stay focused. But because of the continued rejection, Sam began to hang out with the wrong crowd. He wanted nothing to do with God and became addicted to sexting and violent, pornographic websites. Sexting is the practice of sending nude and sexually explicit pictures through cell phones with graphic and perverse messages attached. This is a rapidly growing fad.

Due to his continual sin, Sam had become delusional. One evening he took his grandfather's gun, rushed out of the house, and ran down the street in the middle of the night. He was totally convinced that his family wanted to harm him. This is the kind of effect that repeated viewings of evil and perversion can have on a young person, especially one with Sam's type of disability.

We scheduled a ministry time. Honestly, this is one session that will always remain vivid in my mind. Repentance was at the top of the list for young Sam, and he gladly did repent for going to the dark websites and for sexting. We also led him in forgiving all of his peers who had mocked, shunned, and bullied him. He genuinely wanted to do the right thing and quickly forgave. There was one young girl who was sending nudes pictures continuously. We prayed and broke the power of perversion that had gripped Sam. We broke the soul ties operating between him and this one young girl. As we did, he exclaimed, "Something just lifted off of me. I feel different!"

The Lord led me to lay hands on his head. I was strongly impressed to pray against a lying spirit that was operating in his thought life. I severed all ties generationally on his mother's side and father's side. The power of God moved incredibly as there was a tangible anointing of the Holy Spirit. Sam smiled in joy as he said, "The presence of God is here!" Upon completing the session, we prayed that truth, purity, and an open spirit to the Lord would reign in Sam's life where there had once been perversion, lying, and sickness. I have to confess the Lord did even more in this ministry time than I expected. Sam was radically set free. Some of his signs of autism disappeared from his daily behaviors. It truly was a miracle.

What's Being Pushed?

So what high-risk behaviors might an adolescent feel pressured to engage in? Plenty, according to the Centers for Disease Control and Prevention (CDC). The following are the results of their latest survey.[6]

+ Smoking. By the time adolescents are just thirteen, one in five has tried smoking. Close to 25 percent of high school students smoke cigarettes. Overall, 46.3 percent of students have tried cigarette smoking.

+ Alcohol use. Two-thirds of teens between the ages of fourteen and seventeen have tried alcohol. Of teen boys who have tried alcohol, 20 percent did so by the time they were twelve. Episodic, or binge drinking, is also common. Of the adolescents aged twelve to seventeen, one in four said they'd had five or more drinks consecutively in the past month. Almost a quarter of drinkers aged sixteen to twenty-one admitted to driving after drinking.

+ Drug use. Slightly more than 25 percent of adolescents aged fourteen to seventeen have used illegal drugs. One-third of young adult marijuana users aged eighteen to twenty-one started using the drug by the time they turned fourteen.

+ Sex. About one in every three kids aged fourteen to fifteen has had sexual intercourse. Of sexually active teens, almost 30 percent used no birth control during their last sexual encounter. The average age of the first Internet exposure to pornography is eleven years old. The largest consumer group of Internet pornography is twelve to seventeen years old.

Peer pressure starts at an early age. We as parents and leaders have to do all we can to educate our children, provide stability, and teach them the truth of love and the Word of God to ensure that they remain in the way they should go. We need to reinforce them with the knowledge that they are awesome in the identity the Lord has given them and that this is where they will grow and thrive, not the negative plans of their peers. This is important so that when they are faced with negative peer pressure, they will be able to do what is right.

Positive Peer Pressure

I realize we usually view peer pressure in a negative light. But peers can also be a positive influence. Actually, a teen's ability to develop healthy friendships and peer relationships depend on a teen's self-identity, self-esteem, and self-reliance.

At its best, peer pressure can mobilize your teen's energy, motivation for success, and desire to conform to healthy behavior. Peers can and do act as positive role models. Peers can and do demonstrate appropriate social behaviors. They often listen to, accept, and understand the frustrations, challenges, and concerns associated with being a teenager.

In her senior year in high school, Kendall attempted to ask permission to go with a large group of friends to watch the first midnight showing of the newest *Twilight* movie. In complete agreement my husband and I stated, "Kendall, as long as you have lived in our home, you know the rules. We do not allow this type of entertainment to be watched."

"But I really want to go! Forty of my classmates are doing this as a special senior outing. Can you make an exception just this once?"

"Honey, let's try this. We will not give our approval, but you pray and ask the Lord if He would have you go to this movie. You are eighteen now. You will be in college and making your own decisions next year, so we are going to let you make this decision on your own. The only stipulation is that you pray first and seek what God would have you to do and then base your decision on His answer."

Kendall, not too happy with this answer, accepted it and left the room in a huff.

The next evening she explained to us, "I have made my decision about the senior trip outing. I prayed and feel strongly that I am not to go. I am disappointed because I know waiting in line until midnight with my classmates will be fun. But I am going to e-mail the group right now and tell them I am not going."

After some time passed, Kendall excitedly entered the family room. "Mom, Dad, guess what! I e-mailed the group to tell them I am not going, and several of my friends expressed that they do not want to go either. So we are all going to plan our own fun that night! My righteous and obedient response influenced my friends!"

We rejoiced with Kendall concerning the decision she made and also at the outcome experienced. Kendall is a leader. She always has been. Her friends later admitted that they were too timid to be the first to say no, but when Kendall did, it gave them the strength to do the same.

Is It Possible to Raise a Peer-Pressure-Proof Child?

We know that parents can be wonderful and do the best they know to do, but children and teens will still sometimes make wrong choices. However, we can do things to lessen the possibility.

~ Read the Word of God and pray together.

One of the most important practices we are to be involved in is establishing and building a personal relationship with the Lord. It is also important to create a solid spiritual atmosphere in our homes by praying, reading the Word of God, and worshiping His greatness together.

~ Allow open communication concerning your children's lives and relationship with God.

When speaking with our children concerning their spiritual walks, we definitely need to be steadfast on our convictions and instruct them in this manner. But I have witnessed repeatedly when our Christian faith is aggressively forced on the young without the love, mercy, and compassion of the Lord, the results are young people being turned off and some deciding they want nothing to do with Christianity. So talk with them; allow them to share their questions and concerns. Do not make your example of Christian faith legalistic but one full of the loving, forgiving heart of God.

I know one young boy who was extremely turned off to Christianity and walked many years in rebellion. One form of punishment practiced in his home while he was a child was being sent to his room to read the Bible for an hour. The requirement was then to write a report on what he had learned. He associated the love of Jesus with a strict, religious disciplinarian. Young people want nothing to do with religious legalism and a religious spirit.

~ **Become a soul winner in your home.**

Speak the truth of the Word of God to your children, leading and drawing them into a personal relationship with the Lord. Children and youth are won by love and understanding; speak to them as Jesus would. Here is how to lead a child to the Lord.

+ Explain to them that Jesus is a Good Shepherd who loves and takes care of His sheep. He came to the earth to find all of His lost sheep, to call them to Himself to make them clean inside, and to make them a part of God's home in heaven.

+ Depending on the age of the child, you will want to use words they can understand, so instead of "sins" use "being naughty" or "doing wrong things."

+ Have them tell Jesus they are sorry for their wrongdoings.

+ Encourage them to thank Him for loving them and taking their punishment.

+ Lead them to ask Him to forgive them and make their heart clean.

+ Invite them to ask Jesus to come into their heart and live in them.

+ Ask them to pray for Jesus to make them strong so that they can live for Him and grow up as He wants them to.

+ Help them to thank Him for hearing and answering their prayer.

Here is a simple prayer.

Jesus, I know I have done wrong things like [name some], and I am sorry. Please forgive me, and make my heart clean.

Thank You, Jesus, for loving me and dying on the cross to take
my punishment. I ask that You come and live in my heart and
life as Lord and Savior. Make me strong to live for You and
to become the person You want me to be. Thank You for this
gift of salvation. Amen.

~ Love with the heart of the Father.

I will never forget the time I spoke with the policeman who patrolled
our neighborhood in Houston. New to the area, I wanted to know of
gang and other activities that I should be aware of. He shared about
teenagers in the neighborhood who would call themselves a gang, but
he explained they were just lonely, unsupervised kids. When I asked
further questions, he replied, "These young teens are hurting. Their
parents never give them quality time. They have allowed the television
and other forms of entertainment to raise their young. They basically
are a motherless and fatherless generation who are desperate for love."

Accurate and powerful words, aren't they? We are looking into
the eyes of a younger generation who are desperate for mothers and
fathers—and not just biological parents, but spiritual mothers and
fathers who will show them the way of love, those who will be honest
enough to speak truth and be real in their walk with God. This
generation is not looking for a religion, but for an honest, genuine,
supernatural relationship with a loving, all-powerful God. They are
looking for those who can truly model this and show them the way
to embrace it. When parents' interactions with their children are
characterized by warmth, kindness, consistency, respect, and love, the
relationship will flourish, as will the child's self-esteem, mental health,
spirituality, and social skills.

~ Be genuinely interested in your teen's activities and friends.

This allows parents to know their teen's friends and to monitor
behavior. When bad choices do occur and rules have to be enforced,
parents who have openly communicated with their children concerning
the setting of rules and the consequences of broken rules will experience
less flack.

Learn what their friends are about and what their families believe.

~ Encourage independent thought and expression.

This develops a healthy sense of self, a greater ability to resist peer pressure, and an opportunity to be a leader instead of a follower.

~ Engage in activities with your children.

Whether it be sports, cooking, crafts, or exercise, plan time to do something fun together. My girls love to cook desserts with me. When I make time to bake, they are there in the kitchen with me. Even though I travel in ministry, we love to have special girls' nights. We watch old movies or our favorite "chick flicks." We pull out the bed from the sleeper sofa, and all four of us pile on. We have so much fun. We eat popcorn and chocolate and laugh and cry together. All cell phones, e-mail messages, and outside world responsibilities are forgotten. These girls' nights are highly anticipated.

~ Have your children involved in church and healthy youth groups.

The influence of godly friends and leaders is crucial in a child's life. Know those who are influencing your children and what they believe and teach. A passionate relationship with Jesus Christ and biblical character building in responsibility, accountability, teamwork, compassion, and even work in communities helping others are good qualifiers to look for. These positive influences will take your children far in life. And from a young age through their teens, an "it's not all about me" focus helps them in thinking outside their own little world.

~ Parents, walk in an upright and righteous manner.

Be the example of what you feel your children need in their lives. Let them see you pray and worship. Let them see your failures and how you grow and trust the Lord through these times. Don't be religious; be real.

Building the Next Generation

And it will be said, "Build up, build up, prepare the way, remove every obstacle out of the way of My people."
—Isaiah 57:14, nas

This is a powerful directive from the Lord. When we break this verse down in an expounded manner, it translates:

> Raise up, exalt, highly esteem, give honor and high status with great personal involvement. See and make clear a way, path, journey to a course of life with moral character in raising and rearing our children, our people, our family, our tribe, causing them to grow and mature and to be set apart; causing a lifting up over stumbling blocks, idols, downfalls, offense, or any occasion in which a person can cause a failure on their road in life.

In closing, I want to encourage each of us to walk in a steadfastness of committing our homes, children, and lives to God—walking in His love, bringing an understanding of biblical character, and living in a manner of understanding the times in which our young are maturing. I am a firm believer that knowledge can and does bring power for action. Let's build this next generation to be the history makers they are destined to be and not ignore the battle they are facing every day through peer pressure. Let's be deliberate about bringing a culture of understanding, deliverance, and freedom into our homes and the kingdom of God living in them.

> *Father, thank You for Your incredible steadfastness. We know that there are dangers and battles raging around each of us, and especially our young. We recognize that if we ignore this and do not acknowledge or have this understanding, that inactivity is in itself an open door in the lives of our children. Show us, Lord, any open doors of peer pressure that need to be dealt with and closed. Help us to model Your kingdom in our homes.*

Now to my young friends: If you have engaged in sinful practices due to peer pressure, now is the time to repent and get this right. If you are already struggling with a sex, drug, tobacco, or alcohol problem or addiction, seek the help of a deliverance ministry, your youth pastor, and, if necessary, a Christian-based counseling or rehab program. Do not go another day of struggling with this bondage. Parents, if your child is open, this prayer can be done together.

Father, I confess that I have been involved in [name the activity]. *I repent of this activity and ask that You forgive me. I no longer want to walk under the influence of my peers, but I want to walk in the righteousness of Your kingdom. I pray and renounce all unholy soul ties with all of my friends who have influenced me in a negative way.* [It is important to name each friend by name and break the soul tie out loud. Why? The enemy cannot read our thoughts. He can place thoughts there, but he does not know he has succeeded in his deception unless we voice it aloud or act out on it. He is not all knowing like our God. So say this prayer out loud!] *I renounce all sinful activities in my life, including tobacco, alcohol, drugs, and sex. I break the power of bondage and perversion in Jesus's name. And I ask that You fill me with purity, holiness, and love. Give me the strength to walk a pure life before You. May Your presence become my passion. Thank You, Lord. Amen.*

Chapter 6

The Tragedy of Abuse

THE YEARS OF bottled-up tears from her awful past uncontrollably spilled down Laura's face. From the age of six to nine, she was repeatedly abused by a male leader in her church. This man would meet her in the hallway and escort her into a back storage room. In this dark place he would touch her and force her to touch him. His favored form of abuse was forced oral sex, all the while consistently threatening to kill her or her family if she told their dark secret. Can you imagine this evil, horrific scene that endured for three years? It is almost unbearable to even write about.

Due to threats of violence against Laura and her family, she chose not to tell. Because the agony of the repeated violations were kept bottled up for too long, she now suffers with suicidal thoughts, cutting, anorexia, and bulimia. But through the act of forgiving and prayers for emotional healing and deliverance, Laura is now walking a life of victory and is no longer suicidal, cutting herself, or slowly committing suicide by starvation.

I am not attempting to be overly dramatic as I share this story. The sad reality is that I hear this same story repeatedly in the deliverance room with young people of all ages. Abuse is horrific in any form or at any age. I have witnessed too many times the devastating effects of sexual abuse in the lives of the victims and their families. It is a heartbreaking fact that many of those I have prayed for who were sexually abused as a child were violated by a parent, guardian, grandparent, babysitter, pastor, youth worker, teacher, brother, sister, or even a neighbor.

Truth Concerning Abuse

There are many forms of abuse coming against our young. A report of child abuse is made every ten seconds. Child abuse occurs at every socioeconomic level, across ethnic and cultural lines, within all religions, and at all levels of education. Let's take a look at some startling statistics found on the Child Help webpage:[1]

+ Child abuse results in the deaths of almost five children every day, with more than three out of four under the age of four.

+ Between 60–85 percent of child fatalities due to maltreatment are not recorded as such on death certificates.

+ Of child sexual abuse victims, 90 percent know the perpetrator; 68 percent are abused by family members.

+ Of US women in prison, 31 percent were abused as children.

+ More than 60 percent of individuals undergoing drug rehabilitation report being abused or neglected as children.

+ The cycle of abuse continues, with approximately 30 percent of abused and neglected children later abusing their own children.

+ About 80 percent of twenty-one-year-olds who were abused as children met criteria for at least one psychological disorder.

+ The 2007 estimated annual cost of child abuse and neglect in the United States is $104 billion.

+ Teens who were abused as children are 25 percent more likely to experience teen pregnancy.

+ Sexually abused children are 2.5 times more likely to abuse alcohol in later years.

+ Children who have been sexually abused are 3.8 times more likely to develop drug addictions.

These statistics are devastating. I see these percentages duplicated in my own ministry experiences with young people. Many of them who come to me for prayer have suffered some form of abuse such as neglect and emotional, verbal, and physical abuse. And it seems that repeatedly we are ministering to teenagers or college students who have experienced sexual abuse at some point in their past.

The Growing Epidemic of Prostitution and Human Sex Trafficking

Human trafficking is a modern-day form of slavery. It is the illegal trade in human beings for the purposes of commercial sexual exploitation and forced labor. Many sources report it is the fastest-growing criminal industry in the world and tied with the illegal arms industry as the second-largest criminal industry after the drug trade.[2]

In the worldview picture:

+ An estimated 27 million people are in bondage.[3]

+ Of all victims, 50 percent are children.[4]

+ A child is sold every two minutes, and one million children are forced into the sex trade each year.[5]

+ Of all victims, 99 to 98 percent are not rescued.[6]

+ Human trafficking generates at least thirty-two billion dollars annually for the perpetrators.[7]

+ Internet has made it extremely easy. Craigslist alone makes thirty-six million dollars a year on erotic ads.[8]

This is appalling, but many of you might be asking why this information is being included in this book. Let's look at statistics in our nation for this crime.

+ According to a 2001 report, the number for US children at risk for trafficking is 300,000...and growing.[9]

+ Less than one percent of the cases are solved.[10]

+ One out of three homeless youth in the United States are sold into sex slavery within forty-eight hours of running away or being kicked out.[11]

+ The average age of entry into sex trafficking is twelve to thirteen years old.[12]

+ The life expectancy of a child sold into sex slavery is seven years.[13]

+ Domestic trafficking is more prevalent than international minor sex trafficking.[14]

+ U.S. children normally gain access to social services (trauma counseling, shelter/residential care, medical care, etc.) by being charged with delinquency or prostitution.[15]

~ Who can become a victim?

Reports say that children of many ethnicities, races, socioeconomic class, gender, or religion are at risk for becoming victims, but the risk increases if they are:

+ Abused physically, emotionally, or sexually

+ Poverty-stricken

+ Neglected by parents

+ Left behind by the education system

+ Transient

+ Part of foster care or Child Protective Services

+ Involved in juvenile justice system

+ Throwaways and runaways

+ Living in an area high in gangs or prostitution

~ Pornography and child pornography: an underlying factor

Now what I will share next should absolutely gain our attention and break our hearts. It is also one of the main reasons I am including this information in this book. It is time we sound the alarm concerning the sex trafficking issue, but we also have to understand that it is a problem that has also crept into the church. Here are the facts:

+ More than 100,000 websites feature child pornography.[16]

+ Of all websites, 60 percent are pornographic.[17]

+ Of Americans, 52 percent spend between one to eleven hours a week viewing pornography.[18]

+ More than 32 million people visit a porn site each month.[19]

+ More than half of child pornography sites are hosted in the United States.[20]

+ More than 70 percent of men between the ages of eighteen and thirty-four visit a pornographic site every month.[21]

+ Sixty-five percent of men in church and 35 percent of pastors struggle with pornography.[22]

+ Forty-seven percent of families admit that pornography is a problem in the home.[23]

+ Of US "born-again" Christian adults, 29 percent say it is morally acceptable to view movies with explicit sexual behavior.[24]

+ Of Christians, 70 percent say that their pornography habit is a secret.[25]

+ More than 70 percent of incarcerated sex offenders fueled their addiction by viewing child pornography.[26]

+ Gonzo pornography is now the "training ground" for teaching the child trapped in sex trafficking how the pimps, also known as Johns, want them to perform.[27]

What is gonzo pornography? It is the fastest-growing and most popular form of pornography. It is considered a virtual sexual experience because this pornography brings the camera up close and virtually into the act of sex. Many of the young girls used, viewed, and violated in these films are those being held as slaves in the human sex trafficking industry. The church with its involvement in viewing pornography is playing a major role in the funding of these young girls and boys trapped in this nightmare. Lord, help the church and set us free!

What Does the Bible Have to Say?

In Matthew 18:1–9 Jesus makes very clear statements about how we should relate to and view children:

1. Humility and simple trust are basic qualifications for adults to enter the kingdom of heaven.

2. Those who bless children bless Jesus Himself.

3. The worst punishment imaginable is given to anyone who leads children into deliberate sin.

4. It would be preferable for the party guilty of hurting children to be drowned in the sea with a millstone

around his neck than to suffer the penalty God would hand down.

5. It would be better to avert eternal punishment by physically destroying the part of the body used for such a violation.

Understandably, Jesus is addressing the intentional leading of a child into the practice of sin. The Greek word used for *stumble* is *skandalizo*. It means to put a trap, a stumbling block, or hindrance in the way of another, causing them to trip or fall. Another meaning is "to offend" or cause another to be angry or shocked to the point that they no longer believe or have faith. Our English word *scandalous* is derived from this Greek word, and it is defined as disgraceful, shameful, improper, or shocking, causing reproach or disgrace.

Numerous sins against children can be identified by these words. But when children are deliberately abused, and particularly when the abuse is sexual, the above words expressly and adequately identify this horrid act. I am not expressing this just as a personal belief, but also of what I have viewed and witnessed as the consequences of abuse not only in children but also for many adults who contend with their childhood abuse later in life.

What About Justice?

Of course, if you are ministering to a young person and abuse is discovered, justice should never be taken into your own hands. It is right for justice to be served. The offender should face prosecution and jail time. Absolutely, the laws of the land should be applied in abusive situations.

On the spiritual side, when our young have been horribly abused, it is normal to want to see the abuser punished. Why? Because God made us in His image. In His perfect image, He cannot consider or even think on evil. He explains in Romans 6:23, "The wages of sin is death." Justice is a part of our Creator. He created justice. His nature, likeness, and righteousness within us cries for justice. But we cannot embrace the belief that it is our right to be the spiritual judge. We must leave the judging up to God by the blood He shed on the cross. He already paid the price for our sins and the sins committed against us. Jesus settled the matter so that we can have hearts free from bitterness, anger, unforgiveness, vengeance, and hatred.

What Are Symptoms of Sexual Abuse?

The following are possible symptoms of children who might have been sexually abused.

- Fear

- Anxiety

- Withdrawal

- Slothfulness

- Unhealthy interest in sexual organs or the subject of sex

- Frigidity in marriage

- Hatred toward the opposite sex

- Homosexuality

- Lesbianism

- Prostitution

- Addictions

- Overspending

- Very low self-esteem

- Depression

- Cutting

- Suicidal thoughts and tendencies

- Eating disorders such as anorexia, bulimia, or overeating (gluttony)

+ Anger

+ Bitterness

+ Unforgiveness

+ Thoughts of abusing others later in adult life

It is crucial for us to understand legally what is required of us in these cases. If someone shares with me that he or she is being physically or sexually abused, it is required by law that I report their abuser to the authorities. I inform the person I am ministering to and the family members up front that this is the case.

Healing the Trauma of Sexual Abuse

Erica was a beautiful nineteen-year-old woman but was greatly struggling with extreme low self-esteem and lesbianism. She loved God and was involved in a Christian mentoring program, but no matter how close she drew to the Lord, her thoughts and desires continued to be consumed with other young women. In fact, the closer she drew to God, the stronger the battle concerning her sexual identity increased. The enemy did not want her set free. If the attacks and thoughts grew stronger, then this might cause Erica to halt in her pursuit of God.

It was obvious Erica was nervous. Due to past judgment and shunning by other Christians, she was hesitant to admit to our team the depth of her sexual identity battle. We invited the presence of the Lord into our ministry and prayed that His unconditional love would touch Erica's heart, mind, and emotions. She was quickly aware that we were there to help and not to pass judgment.

She slowly began to open up about the extreme physical, emotional, and verbal abuse she experienced at the hand of her father. This man professed Christianity, but the anger and forms of punishment he unleashed on her and her brother were all out abusive. To aid the family income, her parents began to bring foster children into the home. One was a teenager with sexual abuse in his past. Before long, he had intimidated Erica and her sister into performing sexual acts with him and with each other. Sexual activity between the three of them became a normal part of their life. She tried to tell her parents, but when she did, her father punished her severely.

Now Erica found herself trapped in an overcoming desire to be sexually active with other women. She could barely talk about her father without emotionally losing control. And just as is usually the case in an abusive situation, she could not imagine God being a loving heavenly Father who would truly forgive her for her sins. In her mind, all male and authority figures were mean and harmful, which was driving her desire for women.

As we ministered, the love of the Lord began to overcome her pain. She wept in His presence. I asked Erica if she could forgive her father and foster brother. Out of obedience to the Word of God, she did choose to forgive, but we could still see her intense pain. I asked my husband if he could join us in the ministry room. At the presence of a man, Erica grew tense.

The team and I explained about Erica's troubling past. Greg knew why I had asked him to come. He began to compassionately address Erica. He gently stood next to her and took her hand in his. He began to confess to her, "Erica, the manner in which the men in your family have treated you is wrong. It is not the heart of the Father. I want to stand here as a man in the body of Christ and say I am sorry for your abusive childhood and the terrible suffering it has caused you. I am sorry for how it has caused you to distrust and hate men. I apologize on behalf of men to you now. As a father figure, I want to tell you how beautiful you are. You are a precious young woman who is gifted in so many areas."

As Greg shared the Father's heart with Erica, we watched as the Lord brought incredible deep healing to her wounds. Erica had never been told by a godly Christian man that she was beautiful and talented. With each word that Greg spoke out, her heart and emotions were being deeply healed and set free. What a powerful experience in the anointing and love of God this was!

We then calmly broke the soul ties that were still holding Erica back from freedom and prayed in agreement that the Lord would complete His healing work in her heart. A week later I spoke with Erica. Being overjoyed, she shared, "I am free, Becca. The lesbian thoughts are gone. The constant depression and condemnation that were present in my life are gone. For the first time I feel like a young woman. I even went shopping and bought more feminine clothes, changed my hair, and put on makeup. I feel loved and beautiful. And God's presence has been awesome."

Forgiveness

Many times when people suffer through difficult situations, they are angry with God, faulting Him for the trauma and pain. Their thoughts go like this: "How could God have allowed this to happen to me? If He loved me, why didn't He protect me?" The Bible instructs that our God is a loving Father. His love is more immense than we can ever fathom. He provided His Son to die in our places. We are His children, and He is grieved whenever we are hurt or violated. We have to arrive at the realization that the bad things that occur in our lives are not God's error. He is not the one to blame. Now is the time to express sorrow for being angry and bitter toward Him.

The reality is, we live in a fallen world. On the one hand, the enemy and his demons unrelentingly scheme to tempt us toward wickedness. On the other hand, we have free will, and when we decide to turn from God and embrace that evil, the final result is sin. It is through these unholy behaviors that deep hurts, wounding, and unspeakable abuses happen even toward the innocent.

Is the activity of an abuser permitted? Absolutely not. In the events of abuse, sexual molestation, rape, murder, and so on, the violator must be made accountable for the harmful and violent conduct.

Forgiveness does not mean that the ministry recipient now has to establish a relationship with the abuser. Any action that could threaten the ministry recipient should never be suggested.

Both Laura and Erica received great freedom in their willingness to forgive those who had harmed them. The willingness to forgive is vital to a life of freedom and victory. We must make the decision to walk in forgiveness even before any breach of trust, hurt, betrayal, or violation has occurred. When Peter came to Jesus asking how many times a brother should be forgiven, Jesus responded with the parable of the unmerciful servant in Matthew 18:21–35, saying that we should forgive seventy times seven—in other words, as many times as the offense is committed against us.

Our heavenly Father is loving, merciful, and gracious toward all of His children. We have done nothing that is meriting of this love. Even so, He faithfully extends forgiveness, liberating each of us from our debt of sin, and He asks us in return to be merciful and gracious to those who have sinned against us.

Another sobering truth in this passage of Scripture is the visible anger of the Lord toward those who do not forgive. If we harbor grudges, require repayment, and embrace unforgiveness toward another, the Lord tells us simply that He will turn us over to be tortured. This is not something I desire to go through in my life!

Jesus also said this: "For if you forgive men when they sin against you, your heavenly Father will also forgive you. But if you do not forgive men their sins, your Father will not forgive your sins" (Matt. 6:14–15). If we do not forgive the offenses of other people, then our heavenly Father will not forgive our sins. This does not mean that we are to look for an apology from the wrongdoer, nor do we keep a running checklist of wrongs directed at us. The option to forgive is done before any violation has developed and with no anticipation of an apology or repayment. Forgiveness is a lifestyle choice.

Think about this. As Jesus hung on the cross, He cried out, "Father, forgive them, for they do not know what they are doing" (Luke 23:34). Jesus did not look for an apology from those who were demanding His life. He cried out for mercy and pardon. Jesus's death on the cross institutes redemption for all who will come to Him, even those who have hurt, deceived, or sinned against us. Christ paid for their sins once and for all, just as He did ours. As His followers, we should mirror His model.

Forgiveness breaks the control that hurtful people and situations have on our lives. I also would like to acknowledge the importance of forgiving ourselves.

We have all been affected by awful mistakes leading to anguish and loss. Even though the unpleasant events cannot be wiped out, life-changing lessons can be discovered from the poor choices, which can be a great blessing in our future. But oftentimes we set out to beat ourselves up, resisting to free ourselves from the guilt.

The truth is that Jesus perished on the cross to forgive our sins. Our trespasses are swept clean because of His great sacrifice. The Word of God says that He forgives our transgresses and sins. They are removed as far as the north from the south and the east from the west. If we then decide not to forgive ourselves, we have in effect said that the sacrifice Jesus bore was not enough. Erica had a difficult time forgiving herself because of her intense lesbian thought life. But we took her through a time of repentance, releasing herself, and breaking all self-hatred, guilt, shame, and condemnation. Laura blamed herself because she believed the lie that she did something to deserve the years of repeated sexual abuse. She had embraced a victim spirit. She too was set free as we led her in releasing herself from this lie and embracing the forgiving love of God.

Negative Thoughts

Everyone at some point or to some extent believes lies about themselves, others, God, and His Word and promises for their lives. These negative beliefs can become dangerous because they affect all of our perceptions, decisions, and actions. Romans 12:2 (AMP) clearly explains:

> Do not be conformed to this world (this age), [fashioned after and adapted to its external, superficial customs], but be transformed (changed) by the [entire] renewal of your mind [by its new ideals and its new attitude], so that you may prove [for yourselves] what is the good and acceptable and perfect will of God, even the thing which is good and acceptable and perfect [in His sight for you].

We can see and understand why God wants our minds renewed. These lies and the resulting negative thoughts are made up of attitudes, decisions, agreements, expectations, vows and oaths that do not agree with God and His Word. Unfortunately, the major areas of our belief systems and thought lives are made up of these lies. They usually stem from family hurts and wounds, childhood traumas, abuse, or sins of the previous generations. It is obvious to see where Laura and Erica would have many ungodly thoughts from their experienced hurts and trauma. Laura believed she deserved to die, and Erica thought all men and God wanted to hurt her. In order to see them set free, all lies had to be identified, repented of, and then replaced with godly beliefs.

What Spirits Should Be Broken?

In the case of any type of abuse, a victim spirit will almost always need to be addressed. After being traumatically victimized, thoughts can become polluted and false conclusions and convictions develop. A victim spirit refers to the human spirit of a person who's been violated and has processed the experience in a way that opens up the door for a victim mind-set. Alice Smith explains it this way in her book *Beyond the Lie*:

> When victimization produces trauma, demons often attach themselves to the wounded individual to advance the diabolical cycles of events. The victim's fear, intimidation, and hopelessness are now satanically supercharged. A demonic spirit of victimization has a voracious appetite. It must be fed to stay in place, and it thrives on unforgiveness, fear, abuse, and self-condemnation. Though many victims, especially our children, played little or no part in being victimized, the enemy is shrewd. He'll whisper to abused people that they're at least partially responsible for the pain they've suffered, and if they believe him, they're trapped, unable to move forward and grow.[28]

Laura is a good example of this. She suffered tragic sexual abuse for many years that set her into a trap. She was also sexually violated by her first steady boyfriend, who happened to be a leader in her youth group. In her mind she believed that as a beautiful girl, she would always be abused and violated. Her lie was, "It is part of my plight or punishment for being so attractive to Christian men."

In this situation, rejection, abandonment, and betrayal will also prove to be strong spiritual strongholds. Spirits of perversion that gained access through an unholy soul tie with the abuser will need to be broken.

Inner Healing

Inner is defined as the more intimate, central, or secret state of the mind or spirit. *Healing* means to make sound, well, or healthy or to get rid of troubles or grief. I define inner healing as the process of partnering with the Lord in the cleansing of intimate and secret places of the mind, will, and emotions from troubles and grief. It does not always center on issues that necessitate deliverance, but it does focus on the healing of deep wounds in our mind and emotions that hinder emotional and spiritual well-being. Oftentimes inner healing is needed when there have been devastating repeated breaches of trust, especially with someone who is close. The cause can also be from a traumatic or violating event or an instance when protection from a loved one should and could have been provided but was not. Forgiveness toward the one who inflicted harm is key. In my experience, deliverance and inner healing go hand in hand. It is not an either-or, but a joining together to provide complete healing and restoration.

In this phase of the ministry all *inner vows* will need to be repented of and renounced. A vow is defined as a solemn promise or assertion. It is an act of the commitment of the will to act or serve. In painful and traumatic situations, vows, or what are also termed oaths or inner vows, will be made. An example is, "Because my father hurt me so badly, I will never be like him." On the surface, deciding not to be abusive is right and good. However, when this is done from the place of unforgiveness and bitterroot judgments, it becomes a magnet to the demonic realm, and the exact thing the person is trying to determine not to be is usually the exact thing they begin to become. In the inner healing portion of ministry, repentance and renunciation of these vows will need to occur.

After evicting the demons that had gripped Laura and Erica from their devastating childhood experiences, we led them in a time of inner healing. Asking God to heal and wash over emotions and memories with His acceptance, love, and peace invites restoration. I also welcomed a new impartation and fresh revelation of His love.

It is wonderful to witness the healing power of the touch of God. Are the painful memories forgotten? Usually not, but the sting of the memories will no longer be present, and the emotions will be made whole once more. Laura and Erica were set free and in turn were able to freely love and trust. Both girls no longer struggled with a victim mind-set, nor did they further experience the barrier in their relationships with their heavenly Father.

Closing Prayer

In the closing prayer, I want to encourage any adults who have read this chapter and have suffered abuse to pray the prayer below. The second prayer below is for children and teenagers.

Lord, I confess that as the church we have sinned against You. Sexual sin, pornography, and abuse are running free and gaining more ground. I confess that I have embraced a victim spirit as a result of the abuse I have suffered. I admit I have been walking in shame, guilt, and condemnation and have believed the lie of the enemy that I am and will always be a victim. Forgive me for believing these lies. And now, I choose to walk in obedience to Your Word and forgive those who have inflicted harm, abuse, and neglect. [Name each person aloud.] I release them to You, Lord. I repent of all thoughts of wanting to get revenge and choose to let go of all bitterroot judgments. I confess and repent of all demonic lies and ungodly thoughts. [Name them.] I choose to believe and stand on the promises of the Word of God. I renounce all activity and embracing of a victim spirit and choose to stand on the truth that we are more than conquerors in Christ. We are fearfully and wonderfully made. Your power is in my life. All fear, shame, guilt, and condemnation that have been in operation I renounce, and I command you to go now in Jesus's name.

Spirits of darkness, I break all unholy soul ties between _____ [say the name of each person aloud] and me; I cancel all sexual transference in the powerful name of Jesus. I cancel any control and manipulation between _____ [name each person aloud] and me. I renounce and break all ungodly soul ties between the abusers and me, through vows, ceremonies, rituals, secrets, contracts, or demonic alliances. I break the demonic cycle of abuse and say you are no longer welcome. All ties to the demonic realm are broken now. I cut the unfruitful root of darkness off of my life right now, and your hold is over, in Jesus's name!

Lord, I invite Your healing presence and love. Every place where I have felt abused, victimized, depressed, fearful, and deserving of unjust treatment, I ask that You fill me with acceptance, love, boldness, courage, happiness, joy, and an excitement and expectancy of all the great things You have ahead for me. Help me to focus on Your thoughts toward me, and empower me to walk in a renewed mind. In Jesus's name, amen.

~ Prayer for children and teenagers

Lord, we invite Your presence to come and touch [child's name]. Bring Your love. Cause [child's name] to come to a place of forgiving those who have brought harm and pain.

Lead the child through a time of forgiving. Use language that is age appropriate. Have the child say this prayer.

Lord, forgive me for being mad. I choose to not be mad at or want to make bad things happen to [name of the abuser].

Once this has been completed, then pray the following prayer over the child.

Lord, we thank You for the prayer that [child's name] *just prayed. We are happy that You have forgiven him/her. We break all negative thoughts and lies the enemy has placed in* [child's name] *mind in Jesus's name. We renounce and break all activity and embracing of a victim spirit. You must go now, in Jesus's name. All shame, guilt, condemnation, and fear, we break your power and command you to go. All perversion and lust that were in operation in the horrible act of abuse, we renounce you and command you to go.*

Spirits of darkness, I break all unholy soul ties between [child's name] *and* _____ [say the name of each abuser aloud]. *We cancel all sexual transference in the powerful name of Jesus. I cancel any control and manipulation between* [child's name] *and* _____ [say the name]. *I renounce and break all ungodly soul ties between the abusers and* [child's name] *through vows, ceremonies, rituals, secrets, contracts, or demonic alliances. I break the demonic cycle of abuse and say you are no longer welcome. All ties to the demonic realm are broken now. I cut the unfruitful root of darkness off of* [child's name]. *Your hold is over, in Jesus's name!*

Lord, we invite Your healing presence and love. Every place where [child's name] *has felt abused, victimized, depressed, fearful, and deserving of unjust treatment, I ask that You fill him/her with acceptance, love, boldness, courage, happiness, joy, excitement, and expectancy of all the great things you have ahead. Help him/her, Lord, to focus on Your thoughts toward him/her and empower him/her to walk in a renewed mind.* [Child's name] *chooses to stand on the truth that he/she is more than a conqueror in Christ and that he/she is fearfully and wonderfully made. We say* [child's name] *is loved with Your Father's heart and is walking in the peace, comfort, and security of this love from this day forward. In Jesus's name, amen.*

Chapter 7

The Power of Trauma

J AMES WAS ALWAYS smaller than the children his age and extremely self-conscious. His friends and other children would make fun of him. He tried to bond with his father and longed to spend time with him. Unfortunately, his dad was a workaholic and never allowed time to spend with his son. James longed for friends and quality time with his father.

From a young age, the enemy spoke lies of rejection due to the trauma of the constant teasing of classmates and the lack of fatherly attention and affection. As rejection established a foothold in his life, so did anger, which gradually turned into rebellion. His thoughts were, "God is not real. If there was a God, my life would not be so bad." In order to cover up his pain, James turned toward violence, gangs, and drugs. The great report is that James is now saved, delivered, set free, and passionately seeking God. His willingness to forgive those who harmed him was the first giant step into receiving breakthrough. James is a good example of how trauma in many areas of life will build up a large wall of hurt, rejection, and rebellion.

also body of Christ

Trauma is defined as a serious injury or shock to the body, as from violence or an accident; an emotional wound or shock that creates substantial, lasting damage to the psychological development of a person, often leading to neurosis; or an event or situation that causes great distress and disruption.

Causes of Trauma

As we discussed abuse, we will now look at other areas of trauma that children and youth encounter and the spirits that grip those who have experienced these wounds. While this is not a complete list, it is thorough enough to give an accurate picture of the types of traumas dealt with in a deliverance setting.

~ Conception and throughout pregnancy

All of us begin our life's journey out of a union between a man and woman. This union is meant to be a beautiful bond that produces life. However, there are times when love is not there at the moment of conception and throughout the pregnancy. We find in Scripture that even in utero the young can respond. John the Baptist leaped within Elizabeth's womb when the pregnant Mary approached. What joy John had with the first close contact with the Redeemer of the world! Just as there can be positive experiences, there can also be negative experiences that prove to be an open door for trauma, rejection, and rebellion. The following is another powerful scriptural example of trauma at conception and throughout life. It is the plight of Reuben and Leah found in Genesis 29–34.

The story paints a clear picture that parents can either consciously or subconsciously influence their unborn child. The emotional relationship between a husband and wife is expressed in sexual intimacy and the conceiving of a child. Jacob's sexual relationship with Leah was anything but ideal. His sexual acts with her were done solely out of duty to the marriage covenant. Rachel, Leah's sister, was the one Jacob loved.

At the moment of Reuben's conception there was no love between Jacob and Leah. There was betrayal. Laban, Leah's father, had deceived Jacob, tricking him into first marrying Leah instead of Rachel, the woman he truly loved. To make matters worse, Rachel and Leah were sisters and now competing for the love of the same man.

I believe Leah may have felt rejected, hurt, and probably even bitter at the way she had been treated. However, God saw Leah's plight and blessed her womb to conceive Jacob's firstborn son. Even the name she chose for her son made this clear. As seen in Genesis 29:32, she named the child Reuben, "because the Lord has seen my humiliation and affliction; now my husband will love me" (AMP). From the record, it is clear that Jacob kept fathering her children with no love or support as a father or husband.

It is possible that Reuben struggled his whole life with feelings of rejection. Even as a young boy he felt the need to help his mother gain the approval of Jacob. Genesis 30:14 states that Reuben went out and found mandrakes in the field and brought them to his mother. The mandrakes were referred to as love apples and were used to arouse sexual pleasure. I can hear the young Reuben's thoughts: "If I give my mother these mandrakes, she and Father will eat them. Then Father will love Mother, and his desires will be toward her." But it did not work. Rachel was and remained the favored wife.

As the years passed, Reuben's heart hardened. While a young man, he slept with Bilhah, one of his father's concubines and Rachel's maid, forfeiting his birthright as the firstborn son.

Trauma even at the moment of conception, throughout pregnancy, and during childhood can lead a person into rejection and rebellion. I can imagine that Reuben was so offended by Jacob that in his heart he rebelled against loyalty to his father and polluted himself and Bilhah. Sadly, out of his childhood trauma and the resulting hurt, anger, and rebellion, he aborted God's original plan to bless Leah and him in spite of Jacob's heart toward them.

In *The Secret Life of the Unborn Child* by Thomas Verny and John Kelly, they give this powerful insight:

> The fetus can see, hear, experience, taste, and on a primitive level, even learn in utero....Most importantly he can feel....Whether he ultimately sees himself, and hence, acts as a happy or sad, aggressive or meek, secure or anxiety-ridden person, depends, in part, on messages he gets about himself in the womb.
>
> ...This does not mean that every fleeing worry, doubt, or anxiety a woman has rebounds on her child....Chronic anxiety or a wrenching ambivalence about motherhood can leave a deep scar on the unborn child's personality. On the other hand, such life-enhancing emotions as joy,

elation, and anticipation can contribute significantly to the emotional development of a healthy child.[1]

Another point to investigate is the time the conception took place. Were the parents married or unmarried? Was the mother violated, and was the act of conception done in a violent or aggressive manner? Was the child not wanted from the moment of conception and looked at as an inconvenience? Was the child not the preferred gender? While the child was inside the mother's womb, was there arguing, fighting, or even violence between the parents? In these situations let's identify the following:

Spiritual issues to deal with: rejection, fear of abandonment, fear, a victim spirit, orphan spirit, rebellion. Forgiveness will need to be released to all of those who have wounded the ministry recipient, and all trauma will need to be healed.

Release or replace with: acceptance, love, boldness, power, a sound mind, a spirit of adoption, a loving and submissive spirit, and sensitivity to the Lord. Every place the house has been swept clean, now invite the Lord to fill it up to overflowing.

~ Difficult deliveries

After years of praying for children, it is evident that the manner of delivery and the immediate care following may affect a child. It is quite normal for us to ask about the circumstances of the child's birth. If there was a difficult birth, this trauma becomes the first item requiring prayer. Some of these might include long protracted labor, overdue births, fast deliveries, unexpected births, cesarean births due to danger to the mother and child, children born to mothers with serious health issues, and traumatic instrumental births. Remember, the enemy has never played fair, nor will he ever play fair. At this time of trauma, spirits of darkness will gain their hold.

Spiritual issues to deal with: fear, rejection, fear of injury, fear of pain, insecurity, academic struggles, passivity, low self-esteem, and infirmity. Some children will become hypochondriacs who came into this world in a traumatic nature.

Release or replace with: boldness, courage, power, love, a sound mind, a spirit of adoption, acceptance, energy and strength, and healing and wholeness. Every place the house has been swept clean, fill it up to overflowing with the presence, love, comfort, and peace of the Holy Spirit.

~ A child who does not bond with the mother or father

Most doctors will share that the time following a child's birth is an important time of bonding with the mother. Sometimes babies are separated from the parents because of health issues, or they are premature and have to spend their first few months in an incubator. In some countries, orphaned children are instantly taken to an orphanage, and due to the lack of personnel, they are stuck in a crib and only given human affection when they need to be fed or their diapers need to be changed. This results in children who are emotionally stunted and in the medical world labeled as having "attachment disorder." In some cases, bonding is possible.

Spiritual issues to deal with: Rejection, abandonment, low self-esteem, self-rejection, fear, emotional hurts and wounds, and orphan spirit will need to be prayed through and dealt with and forgiveness released.

Release or replace with: Healing prayers, speaking and releasing the Lord's love into the empty, wounded, traumatized areas of the emotions will also be key.

~ Adopted children

Many, but not all, adopted children have problems. Although most of them know they were chosen to become family members and some might not struggle, there will be those who contend with the sense of being abandoned or given away.

Spiritual issues to deal with: Common problems adopted children will experience are abandonment, trust issues, resentment and anger toward the natural mother, low self-image, worthlessness, and an orphan spirit.

If the child's conception was outside of marriage or the result of a casual sexual partnership, a generational spirit of perversion will need to be dealt with. The insecurity of an adopted child sometimes causes them to become jealous and self-justifying. Rejection, self-rejection, and fear of rejection are common. All soul ties and bonds with the natural parents will need to be broken. If little is known about the natural parents, it is good to pray and break possible family curses and all spirits of witchcraft, anti-Christ, occult, and Freemasonry ties that might be in the past generations. If the child is from another nation, it is wise to do research on the dominant religion of that nation and break all ties and generational influences to all false demonic worship of that culture.

Release or replace with: love, acceptance, peace, joy, hope, worthiness, pure thought life, a sense of belonging, a spirit of adoption and sonship, learning to love themselves as the Lord loves them, a willingness to love and to prefer others, and sensitivity to the Lord. Fill the house up to overflowing with the presence of the Holy Spirit.

~ Children of single parents

It seems to be an increasing issue of women having children by themselves or outside of marriage. In this generation there is a great problem of fatherlessness and motherlessness. Life becomes too busy, parents are working all the time, and children do not get the time they need. It is quite true that there are single parents who do a great job in parenting, and their young have no need for freedom. However, there are also those children who are left to fend for themselves without guidance, affection, and love.

Spiritual issues to deal with: rejection, victim spirit, orphan spirit, loneliness, anger, and rebellion

Release or replace with: acceptance, love, joy, peace, sonship, friendships, and sensitivity to the Lord. Fill the house up to overflowing with the anointing and love of the Holy Spirit.

~ Children of a deserted parent

Travis struggled with rejection, self-rejection, fear of rejection, abandonment, trust issues, betrayal, loneliness, sorrow, sadness, anger, and resentment toward his mother. Why did she desert him? Travis believed the tormenting lie that he must not have been a good boy, or his mother would have never left. He was hurt and angry. "Aren't moms supposed to love their children and be there for them? Why is it so different for me?"

We ministered to Travis and prayed that all rejection and an orphan spirit be broken…that all feelings and thoughts of abandonment, loneliness, sorrow, and sadness be healed by the Father's love. We asked Travis if he was angry with his mother. He quickly replied, "Yes!"

"Travis, can you forgive her?"

"What do you mean?"

"Can you choose not to be mad with her and to not feel like she has to do something right to make up for what she did wrong? The Lord is very sad over what she did. It was not right, but can you choose to forgive her so you will not have to be sad anymore? Being mad at her is not harming her or making her sad. It is harming you and making you sad."

"OK. I don't want to be mad and sad anymore," Travis replied.

As Travis forgave his mother, you could almost immediately see the difference in his countenance. A smile slowly formed across his face. "I am not sad and mad! I feel good!"

We then broke the lie that Travis did something wrong to make her leave and invited truth into his thoughts. It was a joy to watch Travis step into freedom. His father reports he is a happy child, is making more friends, and no longer struggles with loneliness.

Spiritual issues to deal with: fear, rejection, fear of abandonment, victim spirit, orphan spirit, lying spirit, anger, loneliness, and spirit of heaviness (same as depression). Forgiveness will need to be released and all hurts, wounds of betrayal, and trauma of the abandonment healed.

Release or replace with: boldness, courage, acceptance, a sense of belonging, love, joy, peace, comfort, and a garment of praise. Release and invite the anointing of the Holy Spirit to flood in and fill the child up to overflowing.

~ Children of divorced parents

Divorce can shatter children's stability. They can contend with confusion when the family's security is threatened. They begin to battle with choices of loyalty. Often there is a loss of a home and the standard of living. And stepparents come into the scene and have to be accepted. The sad truth is, the divorce rate in the church is no different from the divorce rate outside the church. The lost world is not being represented with a victorious Christian church as a godly example to follow.

Frequently children of divorce struggle with guilt and thoughts of being the one responsible for the splitting of the family. They may suffer with rejection, low self-image due to feeling unloved and deserted, grief, and possible resentment and anger toward the situation and their parents. The following is a powerful story written by Jane Lindstrom in the *Condensed Chicken Soup for the Soul*:

> Soon Tommy's parents, who had recently separated, would arrive for a conference on his failing schoolwork and disruptive behavior....
>
> Tommy...had always been happy, cooperative, and an excellent student. How could I convince his parents that his recent failing grades represented a brokenhearted child's reaction to his adored parents' separation and pending divorce?
>
> Tommy's mother entered....Then the father arrived. They pointedly ignored each other.
>
> As I gave a detailed account of Tommy's behavior and schoolwork, I prayed for the right words to bring these two together to help them see what they were doing to their son....
>
> I found a crumpled, tear-stained sheet stuffed in the back of his desk....
>
> Silently I smoothed it out and gave it to Tommy's mother. She read it and then without a word handed it to her husband....His face softened. He studied the scrawled words for what seemed an eternity.
>
> At last he folded the paper and reached for his wife's outstretched hand. She wiped the tears from her eyes and smiled up at him....
>
> God had given me the words to reunite that family. He

had guided me to the sheet of yellow copy paper covered with the anguished outpouring of a small boy's troubled heart.

"Dear Mother...Dear Daddy...I love you...I love you...I love you."[2]

Spiritual issues to deal with: confusion, fear, fear of abandonment, rejection, self-rejection, hopelessness, spirit of heaviness, guilt, shame, condemnation, anger, unforgiveness, bitterness, and all false responsibility and lying spirits. If the divorce came because of sexual sin, then all generational curses of perversion must be broken.

Release and replace with: clarity of mind and thought, boldness, courage, acceptance, hope, joy, peace, comfort, a garment of praise, freedom from all guilt, shame, condemnation, the truth of the Word of God and the love of God, purity of thought and desires, forgiveness, and love. Fill the house up to overflowing with the Father's love and the Holy Spirit.

~ Foster children, orphanages, child welfare institutions

The reasons why children end up in foster care are numerous. While some families are healed and reunited, this is usually not the norm. Some of these children are abandoned. Some come from violent homes, homes steeped in drug abuse, sexual abuse, and neglect. Or maybe one parent died and the surviving parent does not have the means or the ability to care for a child. While many children are blessed with wonderful, loving foster parents, there are those who do not fair so well.

Whenever children do not have a loving home life, they become independent and driven to protect themselves. Some are emotionally stunted. If they run away, are thrown out by their parents, or removed by welfare authorities because of neglect or abuse, they end up in foster care systems or institutions where it can become a matter of survival; therefore, being the smartest, strongest, and most resourceful is key to survival. The goal of these young people is to insulate and protect themselves from society, which they feel is against them.

Spiritual issues to deal with: rejection, self-rejection, a victim spirit, an orphaned spirit, fear, fear of abandonment, fear of rejection, loneliness, depression, emotional coldness, anger, unforgiveness, perversion, homosexual or lesbian tendencies, suicidal thoughts, and violence. Some might deal with lying, stealing, and bondages such as substance abuse and addictions.

Release or replace with: acceptance, love, a sense of belonging, boldness, courage, power, love, sound mind, spirit of sonship, the Father's love, joy, a garment of praise, life, truth, peace, pure thought life, and all sexual desires cleansed and healed. Forgiveness will need to be released, and everywhere the house has been swept clean, fill it up to overflowing with the Holy Spirit.

~ Family relocations and moves

The five most important factors that contribute to security are the family, home, school, church, and personal friends. When families move, and especially when they move a lot, it may devastate a child. I understand many children are raised in the military and move several times in their childhood and are never negatively affected. But for some, abandonment, loneliness, trauma of always leaving friends, anger, resentment, and rebellion take hold.

Daniel is a believer and loves God, but his childhood was filled with constant upheaval. His father required the family to move every two years. He refused to settle down. But for Daniel, it was difficult. At one point he begged his father not to move the family, but his father refused to listen.

Through the years Daniel quit making friends because it hurt too much to say good-bye. He became a loner. His heart grew hard. In his high school years he decided to turn his back on God. In his wounded state he felt God had continually let him down. He was drawn into Satanism and became a full-blown Satanist. Praise God for praying friends and family. He had a radical salvation encounter, went through a lot of deliverance, and is now seeing others set free from Satanism and the occult.

Spiritual issues to deal with: abandonment; loneliness; fear; the pain, trauma, and depression of always having to leave friends; anger; resentment; unforgiveness; and rebellion

Release and replace with: acceptance, the Father's love, a feeling of belonging, healing, forgiveness, peace, comfort, joy, love, and a garment of praise

~ Sudden death of a loved one

The death of a close family member can prove to be traumatic to children of all ages. Whether it be by natural causes or an accident, death is difficult to cope with. Feelings of anger might be expressed toward the deceased loved one because the child feels he has been abandoned. If the grieving process is not handled in a healthy manner, the child might be gripped with sorrow, depression, and fear of abandonment and death.

Nine-year-old Amber loved her grandma. They had always shared special times together. Even though Grandma had lived a long and fruitful life, it was extremely difficult for Amber to hear the news that she had gone to heaven to be with Jesus. Amber thought to herself, "Jesus, I still want to be with her. Do You have to be selfish and take her now?" But in time, after the shock of losing Grandma, Amber soon began to ask Jesus to look after Grandma.

Soon after the funeral the enemy took advantage of the trauma. Amber experienced nightmares where she saw Grandma's lifeless body in the coffin. This recurring nightmare became a nightly pattern that became all too real. The dreams showed Grandma's dead body coming back to life. The problem was the appearance of the resurrected grandma would change into a horrifying demonic being who would laugh cruelly at Amber, frightening her. It did not take long for a strongman of fear and fear of death to take up residence in little Amber. She became so afraid that until the age of fourteen, her mother had to lie in bed with her until she drifted off to sleep. Praise God her parents heard about the power of deliverance prayer, and through one short ministry session, she was set free and the nightmare and night terrors stopped!

Spiritual issues to deal with: fear, fear of death, anger, spirit of heaviness, and abandonment. If the death of the loved one was suicide, then it is important to deal with hereditary spirits of suicide, rebellion, depression, and death. If murder was the form of death, prayer for spirits of shame, guilt, fear, anger, hatred, bitterness, and revenge will be the focus.

Release or replace with: life, joy, courage, boldness, power, love, sound mind, spirit of sonship through the love of the Father, a desire to live an abundant life, forgiveness, pure thoughts, freedom, and peace in the Lord

~ Children who are rejected by parents, siblings, classmates, teachers, or authority figures

Joshua is a gifted young athlete. He loves his home, the nation of Spain, and throughout his childhood had dreams and ambitions of playing for the national soccer team. However, there was one problem. Joshua's family is Christian. They pray to Jesus and not to "the virgin." Spain is a nation that is steeped in praying to idols of whom they call "the virgin." If you pray to Jesus and not to "the virgin," you are considered to be in a cult. The following is Josh's story.

> My name is Josh. I'm twenty years old. I remember the day I came to the Lord as if it were yesterday. I was seven, and from that day forward my life changed completely. Not only did I find the truth and the blessings of the gospel, but I also experienced the suffering and the battles that we need to endure for His sake.
>
> Since the date of my salvation, He started using me in a supernatural way. The pastor of the church we attended used to ask me to pray for people who were sick and in need. I would pray for them with faith, and the Lord would do the rest. I was eight years old then. And as we know, when the Lord chooses people in their childhood, the devil centers his attacks upon them because he knows the damage they can cause to Satan's kingdom. As I was growing up, the attack of Satan increased. Every day I grew lonelier in a society that I felt couldn't understand

me, a society that would only mock my decision to follow Christ.

Earlier in childhood I played soccer. Everyone had expectations of me becoming a professional player. It was during these years that the enemy used many coaches to humiliate me. They would treat me unjustly when they discovered I was a Christian. They made me run around the field while the others played. They would mock me in the locker room, saying that I was worth nothing and would never become anything. They would put me to warm up in the games because the other parents would be asking for me to play. Knowing that I was the best on the team, they would never give me an opportunity to play. Sadly, I could not enjoy my favorite sport because I was not like them.

It was at that time that I gave my sports life to God. I told Him that if it was His will for me to continue playing, He would have to tell me. Otherwise I would give up the game. My decision was to follow Him, even if that meant sacrificing the love of my life, which at that time was soccer. That day my life changed.

When I became a teenager, demons would visit my bedroom at night, trying to torment me so I would give up in my Christian faith. In the middle of this battle came the pressure of my friends. They all had girlfriends with whom they maintained sexual relations. They would tell all the high tales of how many girls they had gone to bed with. They would mock me because of my stand of waiting for the girl the Lord has prepared for me, and they started rumors that I was a homosexual. Those rumors got to some members of my family. Even some of my relatives believed them and began to ask me questions. This hurt me greatly. I couldn't understand how God could allow this to happen, and for my own family to ask me if I was gay. It appeared I was left friendless. At least that was what the enemy tried to make me believe. In the midst of all that suffering and loneliness I realized that it was worth it to go through that tribulation, because God never left me. The truth is that God was preparing my life for something bigger, and He's still at work in me! The difference is that now the pain of when I was a teenager has gone!

It was in that time that you, Becca, came to our church, and imparted to me the peace that I needed to be able to continue. The Lord showed you the pain that I had felt and how in my past they had called me homosexual because of my stand for Him. You rebuked those words and broke all shame and rejection off of my life. I felt a great deliverance. Today I can truly say that I serve Christ in our church, playing the drums on the worship team, being one of the leaders for the young adult men, and overseeing different cell leaders. Christ never left me alone. Today it is worth it to strive for the cause of God. The Lord said that every one who wants to serve Him must take up his cross and follow Him. These sacrifices are the ones that in our life's walk with God let you know that you have willingly followed our Savior's model.

Spiritual issues to deal with: Heaviness/depression, fear, rejection, victim spirit, and an orphan spirit will need to be prayed through. All thoughts and feelings of self-rejection and self-hatred will need to be broken. Prayers of forgiveness should be released. Anger, bitterness, and all demonic lies that the child caused this will need to broken. All word curses should be cut off.

Release or replace with: Healing from all trauma should be released. Love, peace, joy, courage, acceptance, truth, clarity and peace in the thought life and the emotions, and freedom to express their faith and not be afraid should also be released. Invite the presence of the Holy Spirit to come and fill the empty house to overflowing.

~ Tragic events

Car wrecks, homes destroyed by fire or flood, sports accidents, loss of a close friend, any form of abuse, rape, long periods of financial distress, and violence between parents are just a few of the tragic events that can cause great trauma.

Spiritual issues to deal with: fear, fear of death, a spirit of death, a deaf and dumb spirit (especially when there are accidents with fire or water), anger, confusion, spirit of poverty, violence, or bondage

Release or replace with: boldness, courage, power, love, a sound mind, spirit of sonship, life, clarity of mind and thought, freedom of finances, sensitivity to the Holy Spirit, physical healing, wholeness, and the love of the Lord to wash away all the trauma from the incident. Where the house has been swept clean, fill it up to overflowing.

~ Children of alcoholics or drug abusers

As discussed in chapter 3, this is one of the most common generational sins passed down from one generation to the next.

Spiritual issues to deal with: Individuals who are raised in the atmosphere often struggle greatly with fear, confusion, low self-esteem, and shame from embarrassment and bondage. Due to the extreme behaviors and unstable emotions from living with alcoholics, there are often great insecurities along with a victim spirit and a generational stronghold of bondage. When drug abuse is the issue, bondage as well as a spirit of witchcraft will need to be broken. Drug abuse in ancient times was rooted in witchcraft practices.

Release or replace with: boldness, courage, power, love, a sound mind, clarity of thought and action, love, joy, peace, comfort, freedom and healing the emotions and desires toward addictions, a spirit of sonship, security in their identity with Christ. Then fill the house up to overflowing with the love, peace, and joy of the Holy Spirit.

~ Children exposed to their parents' nudity

Nancy was in a constant battle with sexual thoughts of both men and women. The surprising factor of this story is that Nancy was only fourteen, and now she was driven to compulsive masturbation. It was extremely embarrassing, and she did not want to spend the night with her girlfriends. What if she could not control this compulsion?

The Lord clearly revealed the problem. I asked, "Nancy, do your parents walk around your home nude? Is it normal for you to see them naked?" Embarrassed at the question, she nodded her head as she held back the tears. Her parents were separated at this time, but her father loved to be unashamedly nude. He also encouraged this same behavior in the children. The result was that Nancy was being aroused sexually at a young age toward both men and women, and her constant impure sexual thought life led her into addictive compulsive masturbation.

Spiritual issues to deal with: In this session, we broke the power of generational spirits of perversion/whoredom. We prayed healing from the trauma of seeing her parents unclothed and commanded all shame and confusion to leave. She then repented for the masturbation, and we broke the power of this compulsion and addiction.

Release or replace with: purity of thought and sexual desires; peace and comfort; and all compulsions healed by the Father's love. Where there was bondage, we spoke and released freedom.

Of course, I had a talk with the mother and told her this behavior had to stop. The mother and father quickly complied, and a new level of freedom came into the home.

~ Children who are overworked and who have too much responsibility

Paul's extreme mental illness and torment were obvious. He was an Asian firstborn son, and I was quickly aware of how we would pray. I had seen this before.

In Asian culture, great pressure to perform is placed on children, especially the firstborn son. There is also the cultural embracing of what is called the Korean Han. It is a collective feeling of oppression and isolation in the face of overwhelming odds. It is a state of mind and soul of a deep sadness. Paul had fallen prey to great emotional distress due to this Korean Han.

Paul's mother had recently remarried, and there was now a new stepfather in the home. In his anger he lashed out at Paul one day and harshly slapped him across the right side of his face. Paul was not used to having a father, and now within the first week of his new stepfather's presence, he was violently disciplined. Paul's behavior did not merit this type of aggression. Within two weeks he began to hear demonic voices in his right ear.

The expectations, mental and emotional anguish of the Korean Han, and extreme responsibility to perform and be perfect placed on Paul by his stepfather caused intense anguish. When we met with him, he had been in a mental hospital being watched nonstop. As we began to minister, Paul forgave his stepfather and repented for his unforgiveness, and we prayed healing from the trauma of the harsh discipline. We broke all pressure placed on children by the Confucius belief system. We also broke all baby dedications to Buddha and prayers prayed over Paul as a young baby by the Korean shamans and broke depression and rejection from the Korean Han belief. By the time we finished, the voices had stopped and the confused state that Paul was in had disappeared. He is now in Bible school studying missions.

Spiritual issues to deal with: rejection, confusion, anger, mental torment, all lies of the Confucius belief system, all witchcraft, anti-Christ spirits attached to Buddhism and Asian shamanistic practices, and Korean Han beliefs. We broke all performance expectations placed on Paul and the mental anguish this opened up in his mind. We released forgiveness and healing from the trauma of the physical violence.

Release or replace with: love, acceptance, peace, clarity of thought and mind, truth of the Word of God and the Father's love. We released freedom for Paul to be himself and not what other demonic systems and beliefs were forcibly enforcing. We released a submissive spirit to the Lord and His abundant grace and freedom. Everywhere the house had been swept clean, we filled to overflowing.

Before Moving On...

This is an extensive list, but the truth is, we can add even more. Trauma can be opened through many avenues. Before moving ahead, here is a closing prayer that can be prayed over the above-mentioned issues.

First release forgiveness:

Jesus, we thank You for the price You paid on the cross. You shed Your blood to release forgiveness and redemption for all mankind. Lord, we choose to forgive [name the person aloud who caused the trauma] *for bringing hurt, pain, betrayal, and trauma into our lives. Right now we choose to lay this situation and hurt at the foot of the cross.*

Now pray the prayers of renunciation aloud with your eyes opened and in a calm voice that will not bring fear.

Spirits of darkness that have attached yourself to [name of child], *we break your hold. All* [name all of the spirits that have gripped the child as a result of the trauma], *we command you to go now in the name of Jesus. Your hold on* [name of child] *is over. All lies you have brought into* [name of child] *life we cancel null and void. We cut your power off at the root of this trauma and say that you no longer have power or legal right to operate in this life. We command all of you to leave now in Jesus's name!*

In the cases where unholy soul ties have formed through abuse or emotional manipulation, now is the time to break them.

Spirits of darkness, I break all unholy soul ties between [name of child] *and* [name of each person who caused the trauma]; *I cancel all emotional control and manipulation in the powerful name of Jesus between* [name of child] *and* [name of each person who caused the trauma]. *I renounce and break all soul ties between the abusers and* [name of child], *through vows, ceremonies, rituals, secrets, contracts, or demonic alliances. We break the demonic cycle of abuse and trauma and say, "You are no longer welcome." All ties to the demonic realm are broken now. We cut the unfruitful root of darkness off of* [name of child]. *And your hold on* [name of child] *life is over now, in Jesus's name!*

Now release and fill the empty and swept clean house. Speak and release the opposite of the spirits of darkness that were cast out.

We speak healing to [name of child] *emotions. We say* [name of child] *will no longer be wounded, but the Father's love will come and touch all of those hurt and traumatized places. Where there has been trauma, release Your peace. Where there has been shame, release Your love and acceptance. Where there has been disappointment and hope deferred, we speak and release expectancy, hope, and trust in the Lord. Where there has been depression, Lord, release joy and a garment of praise. Holy Spirit, I ask that You come and flood over and through* [name of child] *from the top of his/her head to the soles of his/her feet with Your love, comfort, and peace. Every place where his/her house has been swept clean, fill him/her up to overflowing. Let Your abundant life reign in* [name of child] *life. Thank You, Jesus, for Your faithfulness. Amen.*

Chapter 8

Words Will Never Hurt Me?

WHILE MINISTERING IN Spain, I shared in a home-church meeting. The pastor's sixteen-year-old daughter sat on the sofa quietly as we worshiped. I felt the Lord drawing my attention to her, and I gently laid hands on her. I wept as I felt the grief this young girl had been experiencing. In the natural, I knew nothing of what had happened, but I saw a vision of what she had been suffering. The following is Lydia's story.

> My name is Lydia. I am twenty-two years old. I have two brothers, and the three of us were brought up by our parents in the Word of God. As children we had great faith and lived in a supernatural way. For me, it was normal to see angels. I remember nights waking up suddenly to see an angel standing at the foot of my bed. His smile gave me so much peace.
>
> When I was seven, I asked my mom a question, and the answer she gave me would change my life forever. "Mom, who do you love more? Me or God?" Her answer shocked me and left me with an ache inside: "Daughter, they are two different kinds of love, but I have to say I love God more, because He gave me everything, including the privilege of having a daughter as special as you."
>
> She knew I would not be able to understand what she was trying to say, so she tried to say it in a way that it would not hurt me. But I wasn't dumb; I clearly understood what she was saying. My mom—the woman whom I admired the most; the one who had taught me so much; the one who would read to me at night the heroic stories of David

and his valiant men, about Esther, Deborah, Moses, and others; the one who made me learn Psalm 23 and repeat it every night; and the one who taught me to read the Bible—was telling me she loved God more than me. I could not understand the fact that she would love someone else more. I cried until she started talking about the great commandment: "Thou shalt love the Lord thy God more than everything."

I vividly remember that night. Since that moment I started asking the Lord to cause me to love Him more than I loved anyone else, more than the love I had for my parents, and more than myself. At first I did not experience anything different, but I didn't give up. In time it was amazing how my love for Him started to grow. I felt like a small flame started to burn as the days started to pass. That flame got bigger, until I reached a moment where I literally felt like I flinging open the windows of our home and shouting to the world how much I loved Him.

At ten years of age, the school I was attending had many new kids, so new classrooms were opened up. They drew lots to see who was going to be placed in these rooms. As God orchestrated it, I was chosen to be one.

When I had the opportunity to witness in my new class, I didn't hesitate. I never imagined the outcome. The children laughed. Whenever the teacher asked me to read aloud, they would insult me, push me, pull my hair, and more. My teacher (who was also new) did not stop them. Instead she would add to the insults and even tried to make the rest of the teachers and the principal believe that I was crazy.

She made me go to the school psychologist (who told me the only crazy person was her! Thank God for that!). As the days passed, things grew worse. They never stopped insulting me. They started screaming that I was a witch and other things. But then they started waiting for me after school hours to hit me. They would bring outsiders who were stronger and taller than me. They even brought their relatives, grown-ups (parents and grandparents). They would gang up against me and scream insults. They would hit me with whatever they had at hand—sticks, stones, whatever. This was all so I would stop sharing about God. I never stopped, though. I continued talking about Him.

My parents didn't know what was really happening, since I would lie about my bruises, saying that I had fallen down. I was afraid of them going to school and talking to the teachers and making things worse.

All of that ended when I started junior high, but my heart was wounded. I had many questions that needed to be answered. I never stopped loving Him, but the doubts and the questions were there.

At sixteen, Becca came to our home church. For the family, and especially for me, she was sent from God. She was in the middle of preaching, when she started prophesying over me. It was so strong how God used her that I could not cry or react in that moment. I was just sitting there, listening. All that God said through her healed my heart. She started speaking about everything I had experienced, how He had always been at my side, but what really impacted me, and what I have kept in my heart even until today, was when she started saying, "God thanks you....Thank you for all you have done, all you have gone through..."

Those words for me are more precious than gold itself. Nothing has given me the necessary strength to continue as the knowledge that God is grateful, grateful for something that is literally nothing compared to everything He has done and is doing in my life, for and because of me.

The Truth Concerning Words

We have all heard the childhood rhyme, "Sticks and stones may break my bones, but words they never hurt me." This could not be further from the truth. Words can be more hurtful than physical pain. I once heard a Christian leader in the underground persecuted church in China say that the physical persecution he endured for his Christian faith in China was much easier to suffer than the hurtful words of accusation and betrayal by his Christian friends.

Proverbs 18:21 clearly describes the power of words: "Words kill, words give life; they're either poison or fruit—you choose" (THE MESSAGE).

The way in which we speak and the content of what is spoken have the ability to manipulate and control the care, well-being, and concerns of others. The manner of communication can grasp or hold one in bondage. Words can and do bring death or life, hope, purpose, and emotional well-being. We have the choice.

I once ministered to a young woman who was told by her parents that she was beautiful. However, the popular boys at school verbally assaulted her in a cruel manner. One day as she walked down the school halls, the most popular boy in her class shouted out, "Here comes the ugly pig!" Bursting into laughter, those around him joined in the name-calling. She confided to me, "I know my parents meant well and what they spoke was the truth. However, I was so hurt and wounded that the enemy began to speak deceptions to me that my parents had lied and that I was not beautiful. This was my ungodly thought pattern. Why did my parents lie? It would have been better for them to tell me I was not a pretty than to make me believe I was. Then when the popular kids at school starting speaking the 'real truth,' at least I would have been prepared." Obviously, this young woman struggled with a victim spirit from the excessive teasing. The good news is, she is now free.

Word Curses

It would be great to be able to report that negative words only come from classmates, but this is not the case. We minister to children and the young who habitually experience harmful words from loved ones and other authority figures.

Spoken words that bring death and harm are known as word curses. A curse is the practice of calling down evil or injury on someone or something. In deliverance ministry, breaking the effect of word curses is common. The entry point can be a witchcraft curse that is placed on or spoken against an individual by Wiccans or those involved in other occult practices.

Consistently repeated spoken words of failure also produce a curse. For example, when words such as "You are not worth anything," "You will never amount to anything," "You are fat," "You are lazy," or "You are not wanted" have been spoken over a child by a parent, guardian, or loved one, this child has been cursed. When words of rejection are audibly spoken against an unwanted pregnancy or child while in the womb, an open door of rejection has been created. Even harsh or unrelenting teasing will prove to be an open door for word curses.

Parents, teachers, youth leaders, pastors, and all who are reading this book, listen to me; we should guard our words. There is power in the tongue. Words should be chosen wisely and in love.

Dean approached the altar with the encouragement of his friend Chuck. I could see the pain on the little boy's face. I asked, "Dean, can I pray for you? Will it bother you if I lay hands on you while I pray?"

In a nervous voice he responded, "No."

I gently laid my hands on his shoulders and invited the Holy Spirit to rest upon him. He revealed to me the cause of this young boy's need and pain. To confirm the revelation, I asked, "Dean, did your father leave you and your mother when you were little? Did he say hurtful things?"

Shyly he nodded in agreement.

"Dean, Jesus loves you. He is so sad that this happened. I am sad that your father did this. Can we pray and ask the Lord to bring His healing so the pain in your heart will go away?"

I knew by the revelation of the Holy Spirit that his father had told Dean and his mother that he did not want to be a part of their lives. Upon leaving, he made the declaration, "I want nothing to do with that boy. I wish he had never been born."

In a gentle voice I prayed, "Father, thank You for loving Dean. He is Your son, and You are so well pleased with him. Lord, Dean is not a mistake. Even before he was born, You created Dean in his mother's womb. Let Dean feel the depth of love You have for him." Tears flowed down that young boy's face as the glorious love of the Father touched him.

I then spoke in a calm voice, "All hurtful word curses that were spoken against you, Dean, by your father, I break those in the name of Jesus. I break the lies and curse that you are a mistake. The power of those negative words are canceled. I cancel the rehearsing in your mind of the words and the believing of the words. They no longer carry influence in your life. I break the power of rejection, abandonment, and an orphan spirit. You are a son of the King of kings. In agreement with Jesus, I say, 'Dean, you are wanted.' You are a good son. Your heavenly Father rejoices in your birth and life. Your identity is in Him. You are free to be all the Lord has destined you to be."

Dean's downcast countenance quickly changed to joy. This boy was free, and he knew it. The power of life and death is in the tongue, but God's healing power can wash away the death and flood His children with love and freedom.

Bullying

Bullying is rapidly gaining ground. As I am writing this chapter, the front-page article of *People* magazine is focusing on the latest suicide due to extreme bullying. It is evident that this is fast becoming a tremendous issue young people are contending with. The following statistics are eye-opening. According to the National Center for Education Statistics (NCES), nearly a third of all students aged twelve to eighteen reported having been bullied at school in 2007, some almost daily.[1]

The report also reveals that:

+ There is more bullying in middle school (grades six, seven, and eight) than in senior high school.

+ Emotional bullying is the most prevalent type of bullying, with pushing, shoving, tripping, or spitting on someone being second.

+ Cyberbullying is—for the middle grade levels—the least prominent type of bullying. It is greater in the last three years of high school.

+ Most school bullying occurs inside the school, a lesser amount on school property, and even less on the school bus.

+ Middle school students, particularly sixth-graders, were most likely to be bullied on the bus.

+ Sixth-graders were the most likely students to sustain an injury from bullying, with middle school youth more likely to be injured than high school students. The percentage goes down every grade from six to twelve.[2]

Additional accounts from the 2007 report share:

+ In 2007, the five worst states to live in to avoid bullies in grades kindergarten through grade twelve were California, New York, Illinois, Pennsylvania, and Washington.[3]

+ Of students, 77 percent are bullied mentally, verbally, and physically.[4]

+ Of those who were bullied, 14 percent said they experienced severe reactions.[5]

Cyber bullying statistics are rapidly approaching similar numbers.

+ One out of five kids on a school bullying statistics and cyber bullying statistics study admits to being a bully, or doing some "bullying."[6]

+ Each day 160,000 students miss school for fear of being bullied.[7]

+ A school bullying statistics reveals that 43 percent fear harassment in the school bathroom.[8]

+ One hundred thousand students carry a gun to school.[9]

+ Of youths who carry weapons, 28 percent have witnessed violence at home.[10]

A school bullying and cyber bullying statistics poll of teens ages twelve to seventeen proved that they think violence increased at their schools. The same poll also showed that 282,000 students are physically attacked in secondary schools each month.[11] The report also states that teenagers say revenge is the strongest motivation for school shootings.

+ Of the teenagers polled, 87 percent said shootings are motivated by a desire to "get back at those who have hurt them."[12]

+ Also, 86 percent said that other kids picking on them, making fun of them, or bullying them causes them to turn to lethal violence in the schools.[13]

The report further reveals that students recognize that being a victim of abuse at home or witnessing others being abused at home may cause violence in school. And that the majority of students say their school is not safe.

This should gain our attention. Our young are contending with forms of aggression, anger, bullying, and violence that have gained strength. I firmly believe that as we discussed in chapter 4, music, violent video games, television shows, and movies are some of the primary influencers for the intense harassment along with abuse and violence in the home. The following is an outcry of a bullying victim that I discovered in my research.

> This guy in my school...bullies me EVERY DAY. He pushes me, kicks me, punches me, and a lot more. I'm tired of it. Do any of you out there have your own personal bully? Because if you do, I'm here for you guys. People who bully people think they get respect for it. Well, they don't. No one respects them because they hurt people.... If you get picked on, just ignore it and walk away. Never use violence. Violence will just make it worse. I'm only twelve, and I'm in sixth grade. I'm a bit small for my age, and I get constantly picked on. So, hear me out people. Let America, nay, let the WORLD know that violence...violence doesn't solve anything. Bye. And bless you.[14]

Responses to Hurtful Word Curses and Bullying

Victims of bullying display a range of responses, even many years later, such as:

- Low self-esteem
- Difficulty trusting others
- Lack of assertiveness
- Aggression
- Difficulty controlling anger
- Isolation
- Cutting/embedding
- Depression
- Rejection

+ Spirit of heaviness

+ Resentment

+ Anger

+ Victim spirit

+ Fear

+ In extreme cases suicidal thoughts

~Cutting

Bullying not only unleashes harmful words, but it also contributes to a devastating practice called cutting. Cutting is done by youth who are experiencing and who continually encounter deep emotional hurt and trauma. They engage in this activity of cutting their own flesh and drawing their own blood in order to relieve emotional wounds. They say that the physical pain distracts them from their emotional pain and numbs it through the release of endorphins when the injury is inflicted. The belief is that it is better to focus on the physical pain than the deep hurts and wounds in their hearts. The endorphins that are released through the increased adrenaline during this act give a rapid, temporary high. This has also moved into what is now termed embedding, or objects penetrated through and embedded into the skin to remain there permanently. The following are statistics concerning this growing fad.

+ Teen Mania shares that as many as 40 percent of our youth have experimented with self-injury.[15]

+ Rates of self-mutilation have been reported to be as high as 14 percent in a sample of 245 college students and 14 percent in a community sample of 440 adolescents. The most common form is self-cutting.[16]

+ In a study of seventy-six adolescent psychiatric inpatients, fourteen (61 percent) reported self-cutting behavior.[17]

According to Drs. Brown, Houck, Hadley, and Lescano, "Most explanations of self-mutilation have conceptualized it as an expression of distress, a coping strategy to relieve tension, an act used to regain control after a dissociative experience, or a product of impulsivity."[18] According to Ruta Mazelis, editor of the newsletter *Cutting Edge*, cutters are often high-achievers and perfectionists.[19] Children who have been physically or sexually abused are also at risk. It is estimated that 50 percent of cutters have been sexually abused.[20]

According to DiscoveryHealth.com, health officials report teen cutting has doubled in the last three years. Andrew Levander, clinical director of a self-injury treatment program, believes teen cutting has reached epidemic proportions.[21] Furthermore, the *Los Angeles Daily News* newspaper claims teen cutting is one of the fastest-growing adolescent behavioral problems.[22] One 2009 statistic stated that over the past year, one in seven females and one in five males have engaged in some type of self-injurious behavior.[23]

The most common age for self-injurious behavior to begin is between ten and fourteen years of age. Occurring across all classes, races, and sex, this behavior knows no boundaries. In fact, many famous people have been cutters—Angelina Jolie, Princess Diana, and Johnny Depp, to name a few.[24] Although some sources state cutting is more frequent among girls, others state it occurs equally in females and males. If cutting is more frequent in females, experts believe it is because women have a tendency to internalize anger whereas men externalize anger.[25]

~ Depression

Depression is a condition of general emotional dejection and withdrawal. It is a sadness greater and more prolonged than that warranted by an objective reason. It is a disorder that occurs during childhood and teenage years and involves ongoing sadness, discouragement, loss of self-worth, and loss of interest in usual activities. The Teen Mania website shares that the use of prescription drugs (Ritalin, antidepressants, and the like) by children/teens has increased substantially in the past few years, and 15 percent of children and teens have seriously considered suicide.[26]

Depression can be a temporary response to many stresses. In adolescents, depressed mood is common because of:

+ The normal process of maturing and the stress associated with it

+ The influence of sex hormones

+ Independence conflicts with parents

+ The death of a friend or relative

+ A breakup with a boyfriend or girlfriend

+ Failure at school

Teenagers who have low self-esteem, who are highly self-critical, and who feel little sense of control over negative events are particularly at risk to become depressed. Girls are twice as likely as boys to experience depression. A generational influence of depression makes children more receptive.

Let's investigate the events or situations over which a child or adolescent feels little control:

+ Bullying or harassment at school or somewhere else

+ Child abuse—both physical and sexual

+ Chronic illness

+ Learning disabilities

+ Poor social skills

+ Stressful life events, particularly the loss of a parent to death or divorce

+ Unstable caregiving

Exposure to media violence can contribute to a variety of physical and mental health problems for children and adolescents, including aggressive behavior, nightmares, desensitization to violence, fear, and depression. Listening to explicit music lyrics can affect schoolwork, social interactions, and produce significant changes in mood and behavior.

Many adolescents with depression may also have:

+ Anxiety disorders

+ Attention-deficit hyperactivity disorder (ADHD)

+ Bipolar disorder

+ Eating disorders (bulimia and anorexia)

+ Self-mutilation

Spiritually they will struggle with:

+ Despair

+ Dejection

+ Hopelessness

+ Oppression

+ A broken heart that will not mend

+ Self-pity

+ Rejection

+ Thoughts of death

+ A victim spirit

+ Wallowing

+ Heaviness

Depression Now a Growing Fad?

Once the enemy gets a stronghold, he will begin his scheme of turning his deceptions into widespread cultural beliefs. This is exactly what is happening with depression and cutting. One of the newest, negative trends is termed *emo*. Emo, meaning emotional, is a term that has been emerging for the past several years. It began in Washington DC in the 1980s as a hard-core punk music movement. It was referred to as emotional hard core or emocore. From there it has continued to evolve combining it with different music forms.

It is very active today and has hit the fashion world with its own styles. As mentioned in chapter 4, music can produce a revolution in culture. This music has birthed what is now termed an emo subculture. This group is made up of youth who consider themselves to be emotionally sensitive, shy, introverted, outcasts, and anxiety and strife ridden. Many are depressed, engage in self-injury such as cutting and embedding and sometimes suicide. These children are suffering emotionally and admit their depression and lifestyle of cutting. Their wardrobe consists of dark, tight skinny jeans and T-shirts. Their hair is usually tousled and dark with sharp angles hiding their face. It sometimes has pink, purple, and blue highlights. Many wear socks or dark gloves on their hands and arms to hide the wounds and scars. Males and females wear dark eyeliner, and oftentimes the boys will kiss each other in a twisted attempt to attract girls. The following is an alarming and sad statement.

> It is a fact that every emo kid has "razor" cuts on their hands. However, one may notice they are always in the incorrect direction so as not to cause death. Some of the more "rebellious" emo kids have razor cuts that go all the way down their arm, also referred to as "cutting down the street." It is also noted that these are usually caused when the emo kids "accidentally on purpose" cut themselves after they're told, "I don't [care] about your problem" by normal people.[27]

There is a hurting generation out there crying for mothers and father to bring them out of hopelessness. If you know of a young person involved in this, pray for them, and get them to a counselor who can help. This is not the type of activity to ignore.

~ What does the Word of God say?

> To grant [consolation and joy] to those who mourn in
> Zion—to give them an ornament (a garland or diadem) of
> beauty instead of ashes, the oil of joy instead of mourning,
> the garment [expressive] of praise instead of a heavy,
> burdened, and failing spirit—that they may be called
> oaks of righteousness [lofty, strong, and magnificent,
> distinguished for uprightness, justice, and right standing
> with God], the planting of the Lord, that He may be
> glorified.
>
> —ISAIAH 61:3, AMP

The Hebrew word for "heavy" is *keheh*. It means heaviness, faint, despair, to be in a state of anxiety or silent hopelessness. But God says that He will give them a garment, a heavy wrap over the clothing also defined as a mantle of praise. The Hebrew word for praise is *tahillah*, meaning a song of praise, adoration, and thanksgiving. It signifies the speaking of positive words concerning the excellence of another.

Breaking the Power of Persecution and Bullying

Amanda sat on the floor of her room. I made my way in to sit next to her. I could see the hurt in her eyes from the painful situation she had been walking through at school. Amanda had always struggled academically and had to work harder than her friends. She battled thoughts of inferiority and therefore never had a lot of friends. She thought this school year would be different as she had made several close friends. But her excitement soon turned to despair as her friends turned on her, began to cruelly make fun of her, and laugh at her as she made her way through the school halls. The new confidence Amanda had found disappeared, and depression took over as the power of the words spoken against her were repeatedly rehearsed in her thoughts. In order to take her focus off of her emotional pain, she had begun to cut herself. If she hurt physically, then emotionally the pain would not be so bad.

I listened to Amanda's painful story and asked her if I could minister to her. Her parents knew she needed prayer and deliverance and had asked me to pray for her. Amanda agreed but was also nervously reluctant about what this would involve. I created a safe environment by sitting on the floor beside her, listening to her story, lovingly talking with her, and in a nonthreatening way began the ministry process. She cautiously engaged. It was evident that not trusting others and not feeling safe in another person's presence was an affect of the painful words and actions of her peers. I asked if she was willing to forgive. She expressed her desire to do this, but her emotions did not match her willingness.

"Amanda, I said, "by choosing to forgive, you are not only releasing those who have harmed you, but you are also freeing yourself from the control of this situation. If you forgive, you can move out of despair into freedom in the healing power of God." Amanda tearfully forgave.

Knowing that she was harming her body, the temple of the Lord, I led her in a time of repentance for the defilement and sin. I then broke the power of a spirit of heaviness and all hopelessness, unworthiness, depression, and despair that had gripped Amanda. I renounced the power of all rejection and fear.

"Sweetheart, are you struggling with suicidal thoughts?" I asked her.

Reluctantly and not wanting to admit it, she responded in a soft, trembling whisper, "Yes."

Again, I led Amanda in a time of repentance for her thoughts of wanting to end her life. The influence of a spirit of death was broken off of her thoughts and emotions along with all the tormenting lies.

The Lord brought Amanda great freedom. We finished by filling up her swept clean house with love, acceptance, boldness, hope, praise, confidence, trust, life, and a joy for living out who God created her to be. Her countenance went from depression and anguish to smiling and tears of joy. Amanda has not cut or experienced a suicidal thought since that day.

Do you see God's magnificent power and love to see these young people liberated? Our young do not have to carry into adult life these pains, abuses, and traumas. Nor do they have to wait until they are adults to receive freedom. If we promote the culture of deliverance to our young and they see that it is not something bizarre or flaky or to be feared, they too will hunger for God's empowering touch.

Breaking the Power of Word Curses and Bullying

Releasing forgiveness:

> *Jesus, I thank You for the price You paid on the cross. You shed Your blood to release forgiveness and redemption for all mankind. Where I have harbored bitterroot judgments against* [name each person], *I ask that You forgive me for seeking revenge and vengeance. Jesus, I choose to forgive* [name each person aloud who spoke the word curses and/or who did the bullying] *for cursing me and bringing hurt, pain, betrayal, and trauma into my life. I choose to forgive as You forgive, and I lay this hurtful situation at the foot of the cross. Help me to love others with Your love.*

Prayer of repentance:

> *Jesus, I realize that You created my body as the temple, my body is Your creation, and it is sin to harm or defile Your temple. I confess that cutting and despising myself is sin. I ask that You forgive me for shedding my blood to relieve my emotional pain. Lord, where I have hated myself, I ask that You forgive me. Where I have turned to pain instead of to You for comfort, please forgive me. Help me to see and love myself as You do.*

Breaking depression: Before praying, I need to give instruction. In this prayer we will bind the strongman and plunder all the activity of the demons it brings along with itself. Then we will evict the strongman of depression. Why? In cases like this, especially if there has been cutting and bloodshed, this gives more power to the demonic. We want to ensure that the strongman is totally disarmed and dismantled so total victory will come. The list is included below.

Spirit of heaviness/depression, I bind you and declare you powerless by the authority given to me in Jesus. I break the power of all bloodshed and the strength it has brought you. Now in the name of Jesus I command all abandonment to go. I break your assignment and declare your power null and void. I sever all ties between you and the strongman of heaviness. I command all bastard curses to be broken now in Jesus's name, and I break you from the strongman of heaviness.

Then move onto the next spirit on the list. All of these are methodically prayed through. As you do this, freedom will come. Once the list is completed, then move into evicting the strongman of heaviness/depression as directed below.

+ Abandonment
+ Bastard (to alienate)
+ Brokenhearted
+ Burdened
+ Condemnation
+ Continual sadness
+ Critical
+ Cruel
+ Crying
+ Cutting/ embedding
+ Death
+ Defeatism
+ Dejection
+ Depression

+ Despair
+ Despondency
+ Discouragement
+ Disgust
+ Disorder
+ Dread
+ Drivenness, excessive
+ Escapism
+ False burden
+ Fatigue
+ Fear
+ Gloom
+ Gluttony
+ Grief

- Guilt
- Headache (or migraines)
- Heartbreak, heartache
- Hopelessness
- Hurt
- Hyperactivity
- Indifference
- Inner hurts
- Insomnia
- Introspection
- Laziness
- Lethargy
- Listlessness
- Loneliness
- Morbidity
- Mourning, excessive
- Pain
- Passivity
- Poverty
- Pressure
- Rejection
- Restlessness
- Self-pity
- Self-mutilation
- Shame
- Sleepiness
- Sorrow
- Suicide
- Tiredness
- Torment
- Troubled spirit
- Unworthiness
- Vagabond
- Wanderer
- Weariness
- Wounded spirit[28]

Heaviness, your house has been plundered. All spirits have been broken and given their eviction notice. I renounce and rebuke your power and say you are no longer welcome in [name of child] life. Get out; go now in the name of Jesus.

What you will find is that the strongman of depression will quickly leave because there is no ground holding it.

Now fill up the empty house:

> *Lord, we rejoice that freedom has come to* [name of child].
> *We rejoice that his/her house has been swept clean, and we*
> *ask that You now come and fill* [name of child] *up with*
> *Your presence. We speak and loose comfort, joy, praise, and*
> *abundant life. Lord, fill him/her up to overflowing, and we*
> *seal the work that has been done here by the blood of the Lamb*
> *and declare victory for* [name of child] *in Jesus's name.*

Chapter 9

The Power of Affirmation

J EREMY LIVED IN a small town in the South that was still steeped in prejudice. As an African American teenager, he felt hopeless. He was not good enough. His family had a long history of financial struggles; therefore he thought he would too. No one ever spoke words of affirmation and encouragement, and now he has a new math teacher for the week—another white woman. Jeremy resolved not to do his work because he felt that there truly was no promise of a better future.

"Jeremy, you need to do your work. Please pick up your pencil and try." Not willing to look at me as I spoke to him, Jeremy crossed his arms and looked away. You could see the years of woundedness and struggles and the resulting defiance in his eyes, "Mrs. Greenwood, I don't need to do this work. It is not going to help me in life. I don't want to do this work."

"Jeremy, I need you to pick up your pencil and do your work. Please obey what I am asking you to do," I replied calmly.

"Mrs. Greenwood, I am not going to do it."

My heart ached as I continued to replay the scene that occurred earlier that day. How could I get through to this young man? That night I prayed and asked God for guidance in reaching out to him. He reminded me that Jeremy had to make his own right choices, but there were also issues in his heart that desperately needed healing. I knew the Lord was directing me to be the one to initiate this healing. I spent time in intercession, praying before returning the next day as the substitute teacher of this class.

As the bell rang, Jeremy walked through the door just at the precise moment he could in order not to be late. I could tell this was a well-rehearsed routine he practiced for this class.

I explained the math assignment. Within minutes Jeremy laid his head on the desk to take a nap while the rest of the class did their work. This was my cue to add action to my prayers.

"Jeremy, you need to pick up your pencil and do your work."

Responding in the same manner as the day before, he said, "Mrs. Greenwood, I told you yesterday, I do not need this math. I am not going to use it in life. I am not going to do it."

I leaned over his desk trying to catch his eyes. In a soft voice I reached out to him. "Jeremy, look at me please. Can you look at me? I would like to talk to you."

Curious, he turned his eyes toward mine. "Jeremy, I realize you have lived in an area where you and your family have been shunned and treated less than because of the color of your skin. Is this true, sweetheart?"

Shocked at my statement and question, he cautiously answered, "Yes, ma'am."

"Well, Jeremy, I recognize that how you and your family have been treated is not right. As a matter of fact, my ancestors were some of the founding fathers of this small town. I realize that some of my ancestors and relatives were possibly some of those who said and did the hurtful things to you, that they might have engaged in some way in the prejudice in this town toward your family and other African Americans. I want to say what they did is wrong. How my race has treated your race is wrong. And I want to ask you to forgive us."

He shockingly replied, "This sounds like church."

"Yes, Jeremy, it does. I also, as a white woman, want to say that when I look at you, I do not see the color of your skin, but I see a handsome, bright young man who has the potential to break out of the cycle your family has been in and to do something great with your life. Don't let the past and wrong actions of the white race control your future. Please forgive us."

Fighting back the tears, he quietly said, "Yes, ma'am."

"Jeremy, do you live with your mother?'

"No, ma'am. I live with my grandmother."

"Does she pray for you?"

"Yes, ma'am, she does. Every night she kneels by her bed and prays for me."

"Jeremy, I know your grandmother wants you to do your work. I know she wants better for you. I do too. I prayed for you last night. I believe in you. For your grandmother and me, can you please pick up your pencil and do your work? Can you choose to make today a new day in your life?"

A tear gently rolled down his cheek as he slowly pulled himself up in his desk, reached for the pencil, and pulled the sheet of paper toward him. As he began to solve the first math problem, he answered in a soft whisper, "Yes, ma'am, I can."

The classroom was so quiet you could have heard a pen drop. I gratefully placed my hand on his shoulder. "Thank you, Jeremy." As I made my way back to my desk, I was rejoicing on the inside and so moved by the spirit of the Lord that I could hardly contain my emotions.

The following four days Jeremy came to class early and would excitedly exclaim, "Mrs. Greenwood, are we going to learn something new today? I am going to do my work."

The remainder of the school year Jeremy would always try to come and find the classroom where I was subbing that day. One day he asked to speak with me. "Mrs. Greenwood, I have friends who want me to hang out with them tonight. They are going to be up to no good."

"Jeremy, are you looking for an adult to help you tell them you can't go?"

"Yes, ma'am."

"Jeremy, you go tell your friends that Mrs. Greenwood said it is not a good idea for you to hang out tonight, and if they have a problem, they can come see me."

I smiled as Jeremy walked out of the classroom confidently exclaiming, "Hey, guys, Mrs. Greenwood said it is not a good idea for me to go tonight, and if you have a problem with this, you can talk with her about it!"

Affirmation Defined

Affirmation is defined as the assertion that something exists or is true, a statement or proposition that is declared to be true. Affirming words of encouragement and love will set the stage for a secure and confident identity. The Word of God shares:

> Affirm your promises to me—promises made to all who fear you. Deflect the harsh words of my critics—but what you say is always so good. See how hungry I am for your counsel; preserve my life through your righteous ways!
> —PSALM 119:38–40, THE MESSAGE

> Whatever God has promised gets stamped with the Yes of Jesus. In him, this is what we preach and pray, the great Amen, God's Yes and our Yes together, gloriously evident. God affirms us, making us a sure thing in Christ, putting his Yes within us. By his Spirit he has stamped us with his eternal pledge—a sure beginning of what he is destined to complete.
> —2 CORINTHIANS 1:20–22, THE MESSAGE

The Greek word for *affirm* is *bebaioo*. It means to cause something to be known as certain, increase in inner strength, and implying greater firmness of character. Our heavenly Father affirms each of us with His words, love, and presence. When He affirms us, it fills us with an abandoned confidence, strength, and resolve to follow Him.

We discussed the negative power that words, bullying, and abuse can have. So, what is the power of affirmation? The following is a powerful quote taken from a Focus on the Family article written by Dr. James Dobson concerning affirmation.

> Psychologist and author Abraham Maslow once said, "It takes nine affirming comments to make up for each critical comment we give to our children." I believe he is right. All normal human beings respond negatively to criticism and

rejection. Conversely, some of us crave affirmation so much that we'll do almost anything to get it.

Children are especially vulnerable to those who use affirmation to manipulate them. As someone said, "Whoever gives your kids praise and attention has power over them." That could be a drug dealer, a gang member, or anyone who could harm them. People with evil intentions know how to use praise to get what they want from lonely kids. This is, in fact, the technique routinely used by pedophiles to abuse their victims sexually.

A highly skilled pedophile can enter a room full of children and instantly spot those who are vulnerable to affirmation. They can have those needy kids under their control in five minutes or less.

All human beings have deep psychological needs for love, belonging, and affection. If you don't meet those longings in your children, I can assure you someone else will.[1]

Building a Godly Image in Our Young

Every moment we are awake we speak to ourselves. Not only do I speak to myself in my thoughts, but also I talk to myself aloud. I do this so frequently that sometimes I am unaware I am actually speaking aloud. My family and friends enjoy listening to my conversations and many times poke fun at me for doing this. Whether it is in our thoughts or spoken aloud, the truth is, all of us do this. So the question becomes, what are we speaking and believing about ourselves? Alice Smith shares this in her book *Beyond the Lie*:

> Psychologists tell us that the average person speaks forty to fifty thousand things to themselves daily. *Seventy percent or more of which are negative.* However, the most exceptional professional athletes are said to reduce their self-talk to twenty thousand or fewer statements, and less than 50 percent are negative. Focused positive thinking and

self-talk are critical if you are to move from victimization to victory. Why? Because "faith comes by hearing" (Rom. 10:17, NKJV). Your belief system is built on what you think and what you say to yourself and not just what you say aloud.

This is why the words of your mouth (what you say to others), the meditations of your heart (what you say to yourself), and the words of others (who you listen to), whether positive or negative, greatly determine what you think, what you do, and who you'll eventually become. *Your self-talk should always be acceptable to God.*[2]

Ras and Bev Robinson, in their book *Convergence of Quantum Physics, Scripture and Prophecy*, share about an interesting experiment performed by scientist Masaru Emoto.

"[Masaru Emoto] wanted to know how the molecular structure of water is affected by our words and thoughts. His findings were astounding and I explain them below.

1. "He took pure water and placed .5 cc each in fifty petri dishes, and froze them to -25 degrees C for three hours.

2. "Then he put them in a refrigerator at -5 degrees C with a microscope set up with a camera attached to take photographs of each of the fifty water drops.

3. "First there were photographs taken of water that did not have information put in them.

4. "Then they took the water that did have information put in, and performed the same procedure just described.

5. "Photographs were taken before and after, and the differences compared.

[handwritten margin note] "Let the words of my mouth + the meditation of my heart be acceptable to You O God"

6. "When they spoke of projected feelings of love and thanks to the water, it formed the most beautiful crystals.

7. "There were pictures of water from the polluted Fujuwara Lake taken before a blessing was spoken over it. The first water shows malformed crystals. After blessings were spoken, beautiful crystals formed.

8. "If thoughts and words can do that to water, imagine what they do to us. Seventy to 90 percent of our bodies are water.

9. "This proves people's prayers and thoughts can affect reality.

"Emoto even had printed blessings taped to bottles of distilled water and left them overnight. Photographs were taken of these with the same procedures as described above. The same results occurred as with the spoken words."[3]

The same is true for our young. What they are saying, thinking, and believing concerning themselves are shaping their failures and successes. Our young can pollute themselves or cause beautiful life by their thought patterns and spoken words. How do we instruct them to accept, believe in, and affirm themselves?

- Teach your young to think positively about themselves.

- Teach them the truth of the blessings from God's Word.

- Teach them their identity in the Lord.

- Bring instruction that negative thinking can harm, but positive thoughts and beliefs bring life.

- Teach the power of prayer.

- Don't let them compare themselves to others, but train them to see their own strengths and to be happy with who they are.

- Praise appropriate behavior.

- Encourage your child to have short-term and long-term goals. Instill the belief that these goals will be accomplished.

- Show affection to your child. Give a lot of hugs.

- Say "I love you," and do not be stingy with these exchanges.

- Have fun and laugh with your child.

- Give your child a few positive words they can repeat concerning themselves. Base these on Scripture.

- If your child frequently says, "I can't," help him to change, saying and believing, "I can!"

- Regularly discuss positive thinking and self-talk with your child.

- Help your child see there is always a new idea or solution to any problem.

- Instead of letting your child become upset when a failure is experienced, bring guidance toward more positive thoughts, ideas, and images. Don't allow dwelling on what happened. Show how learning can occur from the experience, and move on to better things.

Kingdom Identities

If our young are made for affirmation, then they should receive this treatment within their homes, churches, and from their loved ones. Let's be the ones to influence our youth with words and actions. We can do so by instilling what I term kingdom identities. These are truths and beliefs, decisions, attitudes, agreements, expectations, and vows that agree with God, His Word, and our identity in Him. Romans 10:17 shares: "Faith comes by hearing, and hearing by the word of God" (NKJV).

Faith means the conviction of the truth of anything, a belief. Therefore, faith or our beliefs are built by what we hear, see, and experience. As previously discussed, words bring life or death. In order to see our children raised into their complete potential, they must hear affirming words to build their confidence and security. How do we achieve this? Let's put this into practical steps.

~ For children

First, set aside an hour of time to spend with your child. Have a paper and pencil handy. Open in prayer. Invite the presence of the Holy Spirit. Begin your time by sharing that this will be a fun exercise and lesson that will build hope, strength, faith, and agreement with God in their thoughts and lives. Explain the definition of negative thoughts as discussed in chapter 6 and also kingdom identities as explained above. Use the "Negative Thoughts About Ourselves (for Children)" list in the resources section on my website. Have your child put a mark next to the thoughts that they feel applies to their thought life and beliefs. Keep in mind that this is not a comprehensive list. It is to help identify the possible areas of negative thinking.

After identifying the negative thought patterns, take your child through a time of repentance for believing these lies. Then, as the parent, repent for anything you have done that might have added to those negative thought patterns.

Once this has been completed, pull out a sheet of paper and title it "My Kingdom Identity." Write the opposite of the negative thoughts on this piece of paper. Using Scripture is great. For guidance with this, go to the resource tab on my website and select "Scripture Promises of Kingdom Identity." For young children, you will want to keep these in a language they can relate to. For example, if a child is struggling with the negative thought of "I am sad a lot," the kingdom identity thought would be, "God gives me joy in my heart. He wants me to be happy!" Then take that piece of paper of negative thoughts, write a big X across the entire page, tear it up, and throw it away. Make this declaration aloud, "These negative thought patterns are no longer a part of [child's name] identity. Today is a day of discovering and believing true kingdom identity!"

Continue to make a list of kingdom identities and make these a regular focus of your child's new belief system. For instance, they might say them aloud before they go to bed or before leaving for school in the morning. You might make new and colorful posters to hang on your child's walls so they can see, read, and have on the forefront of their mind their new and true identity in Christ.

~ For teenagers

Set aside time to speak with your teenager. Again, have paper and pencils handy. There has to be an understanding with your teenager of the necessity to engage in this process. You cannot force something if your teenager is not going to do it of her own free will. So you want to invite her into this process by being real and transparent. Explain that this is a time to discover and learn areas of thought lives that need to be changed and renewed.

Communicate with your teenager about the lies of the devil and negative thoughts section from chapter 6 and kingdom identities from above. Be transparent and share areas that you yourself are overcoming. Let her know you also are in process. After all, if our relationships are on track and right with God, we all are to some degree or level, growing, overcoming, and gaining freedom. This will create a safe environment and also won't make her feel like she is being targeted. (Do not make this a time to share about dark sins such as pornography, adultery, or even a fantasy life. This is not ever appropriate to share with your teenager. If you have these sin issues, now is the time for you to be calling a deliverance ministry team for help.)

Ask your teen if she feels like she battles with negative thoughts. Some teenagers who are secure and not struggling might not need this exercise. But for those who are struggling, if they are being truthful, the answer should be yes.

Next, go to the resources tab on my website and select the "Negative Thoughts About Ourselves (for Teenagers)" list or already have a copy ready. Give your teenager time to go through the page marking an X by all the thought patterns that apply to her. Together go over the answers. Take the time to lead her through repentance. Pull out a sheet of paper and write at the top "My Kingdom Identity." List a new kingdom identity for every negative thought pattern she is combating. For instance, where she once believed, "I do not belong. I feel like an outcast," write as a new belief on the kingdom identity page: "I belong to Jesus. I am always loved by Him!" Or, "Jesus is my friend and will give me good friends!" Then destroy that piece of paper and make this declaration aloud, "These negative thought patterns are no longer a part of [teenager's name] identity. Today is a day of discovering and believing her true kingdom identity."

Make this a daily part of your teen's new belief system until this identity becomes a reality, where she actually knows and believes her new identity and begins to live from this kingdom position of belonging. Some teens might want to make posters to put on their walls. My two sixteen-year-old daughters enjoy this type of thing. Others may want to journal their kingdom identity, allowing God to speak further concerning His truth and love. Have a family time where everyone shares their kingdom identities aloud. Pray in agreement, welcoming these new beliefs to take root in each life. Trust me; as time passes, these identities will bring hope, joy, faith, and confidence in God's goodness.

The Power of Blessing

It has been stated by many ministers that we are living in the midst of a fatherless generation, meaning that most of the young who struggle have not had a positive experience with their fathers and only some with their mothers. Or if the experience has not been negative, there still has not been the aspect of blessing and affirmation. Maybe affirming words have been few and far between. The first thing our heavenly Father did after He created Adam and Eve in the garden was to release the

Father's blessing: "God blessed them: 'Prosper! Reproduce! Fill Earth! Take charge!'" (Gen. 1:28, The Message).

The Hebrew word for *bless* is *barak*. It means to commend; to speak words invoking divine favor with the intent of favorable circumstances; to speak words of excellence or to meet another with a positive verbal exchange.

Our heavenly Father created mankind because He has a father's heart. He wanted sons and daughters, children in His image to relate to. He desired a family. Therefore He understood the significance of blessing. Starting with Adam and Eve, we see the pattern of blessing throughout Scripture. The Lord blessed Noah, Abraham, and Moses. The fathers of the Old Testament blessed their sons. Jesus blessed the disciples. Paul blessed Timothy. One of the key practices that needs to occur with our young is the affirmation of a father's and mother's blessing—not only speaking the words but also backing them up with physical actions and affection.

Releasing the Father's and Mother's Blessing

In the closing prayer, the focus will be to invoke the father's and mother's blessing. The following is a blessing to be spoken aloud over your children. Of course, you can add even more to the prayer as the Lord leads. The purpose is to release and speak the blessings of the Father into the next generation. This blessing can also be spoken over children and youth who are in need of a blessing that they will not receive from their own mother and father.

> *My child, I love you! You are exceptional. You are a gift and treasure from God. I thank God for permitting me to be your father (or mother). I bless you with the healing of all wounds of rejection, neglect, and abuse that you have endured. I bless you with bubbling-over peace—the peace that only the Prince of peace can give, a peace beyond comprehension. I bless your life with fruitfulness—good fruit, much fruit, and fruit that remains. I bless you with the spirit of sonship. You are a son*

(or daughter) of the King of kings. You have a rich inheritance in the kingdom of God.

I bless you with success. You are the head and not the tail; you are above and not below. I bless you with health and strength of body, soul, and spirit. I bless you with overflowing successfulness, enabling you to be a blessing to others. I bless you with spiritual influence, for you are the light of the world and the salt of the earth. You are like a tree planted by rivers of water. You will thrive in all your ways.

I bless you with a depth of spiritual understanding and an intimate walk with your Lord. You will not stumble or falter, for God's Word will be a lamp to your feet and a light to your path. I bless you with pure, edifying, encouraging, and empowering relationships in life. You have favor with God and man. I bless you with abounding love and life. I bless you with power, love, and a sound mind. I bless you with wisdom and spiritual gifts from on high. You will minister God's comforting grace and anointing to others. You are blessed, my child! You are blessed with all spiritual blessings in Christ Jesus. Amen!

Chapter 10

Delivering Our Children From the Evil One

HILDREN ARE A tremendous gift. Securing their freedom from demonic influence and healing from traumas and wounds from an early age will empower them for kingdom destiny. I will say it again now. There is no reason why our young have to wait to receive freedom until their adult years. Let's see them walking in the fullness of liberty now.

I will say the young are easier to minister to. They carry a childlike faith and do not have years of religious opinions to hinder their ability in receiving from the Lord.

Parents Ministering to Their Young

Parents cannot minister freedom to their children unless they themselves have been set free. I once prayed for a young girl whom we will call Kim. She was in an intense battle in her mind. Her thought life was gripped by fear. We would get her to a place of freedom, and by the next ministry session she was worse than when she left us a week before. She suffered from a severe case of OCD (obsessive-compulsive disorder).

Her parents wanted to see her set free and felt that her issue was spiritual. It was no wonder. Her mother also suffered from OCD, so much so that no one was allowed to even step foot into their home. She was laying hands on and praying for Kim in between the ministry sessions.

I counseled the parents that this child needed to see a psychiatrist. The parents refused to take their child to the doctor. When the severity of the mother's condition was revealed through a friend of Kim to myself and two other ministry leaders, we spoke with the parents and shared the need for their own personal deliverance. They were offended and refused further help for themselves or their daughter. We were so grieved. It was difficult to see Kim and the family live in chaos.

So How Do We Minister Freedom?

When praying for young children, it is necessary to pray in a way that will not cause fear. This should be a freedom encounter, not one that causes further harm. The following are guidelines.

~ Begin by reading *The Little Skunk*.

This is a great children's book written by Sue Banks. It tells the story of three children and the spiritual problems they struggle with, such as anger, fear, and gluttony. A skunk comes into the home while the mother is away shopping. This skunk leaves his wonderful scent while running terrified throughout the house. During this emotionally heightened incident, each child's spiritual problem fully shows itself. They decide to pray and ask God to help get that smelly skunk out of the house. God answers, and the skunk almost immediately bolts out of the house being chased by the cat! That evening their father explains to each child how their spiritual issues are like the stinky skunk. It makes them not smell good. But if they pray, Jesus can heal them and set them free just as the skunk was removed from the house. It is a great tool for preparing children for deliverance.

~ Explain that Jesus prayed for children.

Share with your child that in the Bible parents brought their children to Jesus for Him to set them free from things that bothered them. This is why you want to pray for them and ask Jesus to help. Take the time to share what is about to happen. Remember, you can also pray over your children in the night hours. For toddlers and the young actively on the go, this is the suggested mode of ministry. It will still bring deliverance, but they are peacefully resting while the ministry is occurring. The following is a powerful example of the effectiveness of praying over children while they sleep.

~ Break the generational influence of fear and rejection.

I shared in chapter one my story of being bound by fear and overcoming it. Remember, the enemy will never play fair. Even though I had been set free and had told that spirit of fear it would not come on my children, it, along with rejection, attempted to visit our youngest child, Katie, at the age of five. We watched her go from a confident little girl to being afraid. She would voice concerns that she was not good enough or as smart as her sisters. I could see sadness and insecurity trying to establish a hold in her life.

Per our normal routine, Greg and I would pray for her as we tucked her in bed at night. But after she drifted off to sleep, I began to pray over her in the night hours for a period of a week. I did not tell Katie I was doing this. After a few days the changes became obvious. One evening as I finished her bedtime prayers, she smiled a big, dimple-filled grin and hugged my neck really tight. She asked, "Momma, have you been praying for me while I'm asleep?" Surprised by the question, I answered, "Yes, baby. I have been praying for you." "Well, momma I really like it when you do that. I sleep really good and do not have bad dreams and see scary things. I love you, Momma. Thank you!" I hugged her back and kissed her chubby cheek. "I love you too, baby, and so does Jesus!" As I left her room, tears streamed down my face at the goodness of God to our children and the spiritual awareness and sensitivity He has blessed them with.

~ Be cautious of the word *demons*.

Use words like *spiritual influences* or *bad things* when talking to your younger children. If you focus too much on the word *demons* and *darkness*, this might further frighten your child.

~ Tell the child what you are going to do.

Explain that you might lay hands on them and that you are going to break the power of these bad things and make them leave. Once you have shared what is going to happen, your child should be at peace with the process. You can sit the child in your lap or in their favorite chair. Now remember that young children are not going to want to sit still for long periods of time. We have ministered to children as they have moved about us and the chairs. Keep in mind that for children who are not going to sit still for a two-hour ministry session, you will want to be to the point.

How Do You Pray?

Write a list of the obvious problems that the child has been encountering, for example, fear, rejection, a lying spirit, or spirit of anger. Be sure to cover generational influences that the parents have dealt with. Also include generational issues in the grandparents and family lines on both sides of the family. All known family involvement in the occult, Freemasonry, Eastern Star, Wicca, witchcraft practices, and Eastern religions will need to be dealt with. Strongholds of witchcraft and rebellion, anti-Christ spirits, spirits of error, and lying spirits are some of the spirits to address.

Pray with your eyes open. When dealing in deliverance, you want to pray from a position of authority. Pray in a calm voice and conversational manner. Do not yell or raise your voice. Smile and make eye contact with the child.

In the name of Jesus, bind, break, and loose each spirit you have listed. When you are binding, it is rendering powerless the demonic influence. When you break the power of the spirit, it is preventing it from further oppression to your child. When you loose it or command it to go, the spirit releases the child and leaves. Remember that deliverance is easier with most children. Sometimes while you are praying, the child may cough, sigh, yawn, or even burp. This is a physical sign that breakthrough is occurring. If this is not happening, do not be concerned that your child is not receiving freedom. Sometimes there are physical reactions, and other times there are not. Physical reactions are not the goal. Freedom is the goal!

~ Process of filling the empty house

At this point ask the Lord to cleanse every part of the child where the spirit attached itself. This usually includes the mind, will, and emotions. At times this will also include the physical body, especially true if the spirits dealt with involved sexual sin, infirmity, or witchcraft.

Invite the Holy Spirit to fill the child with His love. Just as shown in chapter 7, this is where you pray, release, and replace with the exact opposite of the demonic spirit, emotional wound, or negative thought patterns. If there was fear, release and speak boldness, courage, love, power, and a sound mind. Release a spirit of adoption and sonship. Ask the Lord to fill the child to overflowing with joy, peace, comfort, and faith. Below is a sample prayer of walking your child through deliverance. In the appendix in the back of the book, there is an extensive list of strongmen and the demons that go along with them. This will be a helpful guide as you pray.

In the name of Jesus, I [or we if both parents are praying] *take authority over all bad spiritual influences. Unbelief* [or name of spirit you are addressing], *I rend you powerless in the life of* [child's name]. *I bind your power right now. I break your influence, power, and lies off of* [child's name] *mind, will, and emotions. I break all generational curses and influences of a spirit of unbelief passed down the family line to* [child's name]. *We sever all ties to you on both sides of the family all the way back to Adam and Eve. We command you to loose* [child's name] *from your grip. We cast you out and say go now! We speak cleansing of* [child's name] *mind, will, emotions, imaginations, thought patterns, and thought life.*

Lord, we ask that You come and bring Your peace, the Father's love, and acceptance into [child's name] *life. Holy Spirit, fill him/her up to overflowing. Cause his/her path to be faith-filled and secure. We speak in agreement that all the plans and purposes You have for* [child's name] *life will come to pass. Now we seal the work that has been done here by the blood of the Lamb. In Jesus's name, amen!*

If there is a need and where it is appropriate, ask the Lord for physical healing. Do not demand, but ask in faith. Then pray for special needs the child has expressed. For example, "Lord, I thank You that Joey has nothing more to fear. You are with him even in the night

hours. You will never leave him. We ask that You send Your angels to
be in his room and that Joey will be aware of Your presence and their
presence."

~ Put the new Kingdom Identity list from chapter 9 into action.

If you have not formed a Kingdom Identity list with your child,
now is a good time to do so. If you have already done this, pull it out
and lead your child in reading it aloud. Find a time where it fits into
your schedule as a family, and speak these truths aloud to secure them
as a part of your child's kingdom identity. As the parent, while your
child is sleeping you can slip into their room at night and speak these
kingdom identities.

Ministering to Your Teens

Basically the procedure is the same, except your teen will have the
ability to understand things on a deeper level. There will be more
openness and freedom to explain the causes of the demonic oppression.
Let's examine the areas that will be different when ministering to your
teen.

~ Generational influences

Your teen will be very aware of the sin issues and the negative beliefs
that you, your spouse, and grandparents have struggled with. There is
freedom to discuss in length the truth concerning generational curses
and that they can be broken.

~ The responsibility of personal sin choices

If the teen has fallen into rebellion, lying, substance abuse, sexual
sin, cutting, occultism, vampirism, and witchcraft, then he or she
needs to understand the reality of the open doors to the demonic these
sins have allowed. It is important to explain that it is time to plunder
the root issues of darkness.

If you suspect or know your teen has been sexually active, it is wise
to teach on the devastating impact soul ties can have when there is sex
outside of marriage. Give your teen the definition of soul ties from
chapter 3. Explain that when soul ties are formed, the demonic from

the other party has access to him and vice versa. If there has been more than one sexual partner, then soul ties have formed with every individual, and all of their demonic issues and negative beliefs will have access. Your teen will need to repent for the rebellion and sin and every sexual partner he has encountered. Soul ties will need to be broken and renounced.

Now, for a teen to be this transparent with parents would be pretty amazing. However, this teaching on soul ties will reveal the truth to him. If he does not want to confess all of this to the parent, then get him to a good deliverance ministry to receive freedom. Remember, the teen has to want to be a part of this process.

~ Speak truth in love and boldness

It is essential that you are able to speak truth to your teen in love and boldness. Do not get confrontational. This is not the time to engage in a disagreement. If you feel you will not be able to minister to your teen without a debate or argument, then send him or her to a deliverance ministry. You want the ministry setting to bring freedom, not more harm. Your teen needs to know you are there to work with him. If your teen will not be able to make it through the prayer time without arguing, then you are not the one to minister to him.

Deliverance Team Ministry to the Next Generation

Now that we have learned how to minister deliverance in the home, let's explore how things will unfold in a deliverance team ministry setting.

~ Children from birth to age twelve

It is good for at least one parent to go through deliverance in order to help the child walk out and maintain his or her freedom. Why? A parent cannot help their child overcome a spiritual issue they themselves have not overcome. All generational doors over the parent's life need to be shut in order for the child to be able to receive their complete deliverance. This is true while the child is living at home. Once a child moves out on his own, a parent's deliverance is not required for that child to receive breakthrough. This rule applies only while the children are still under the daily supervision and authority of their parents.

If the child is saved but living in a home with unsaved parents or those who want nothing to do with church or growing in their personal walk with God, she can still go through deliverance. However, it is important that there is a support system in place and spiritual mothers or fathers to help the child walk out her freedom in spite of the parents' spiritual condition.

When praying for children twelve years and younger, it is good to have the parents present unless they will hinder the child's freedom. Generally speaking, this brings the child a feeling of safety. Ministry settings absolutely have to be a safe environment.

It is important for a parent to be there to repent of any generational sin and to learn what the child has received so he or she can help the child walk out the deliverance. If there is more than one child in the family, each child should go through deliverance separately unless the children are close in age and have similar issues. For younger children, having a sibling in the room leading the way can prove to be helpful.

Tools for effective ministry

As previously stated, the book *The Little Skunk* is a great tool to use with young children in order to teach the concept of deliverance. Begin the session by reading this book to the child.

If needed, use the children's questionnaire from the resource tab on our ministry website. We use this some of the time, but not for every child. Often the issues to pray through are obvious and do not require this in-depth approach. But at times this is necessary. For those who are new to ministering, the questionnaire proves to be an effective and thorough guide.

Team dynamics

Team ministry is important. It is unusual for me to pray for a child or youth by myself. I do make exceptions when I have a close relationship with the family asking me to minister. But as a general rule, two to three other team members are present. These team members need to be trained in the importance of how to interact with children. The following are good characteristics:

+ Very discerning

+ Young at heart and able to relate well to children

+ Free from self-consciousness

+ Free from a religious spirit

+ Able to confront

Sometimes there has to be discussions with the parents concerning discipline, parenting styles, communication, programs they allow the children to watch, and games they are allowed to play. Basically, we are helping them put certain rules into place that may be more productive. The team member also needs to have:

+ Great wisdom

+ Ability to communicate well

+ Freedom to laugh, have fun, and be spontaneous

+ Ability and authority to cast out a spirit in a calm voice with a smile

+ Sensitivity to be led by the Holy Spirit

Under no circumstance should a children's deliverance minister raise their voice to a child. The experience must never be a frightening one, as fear can grip the child and add further demonic influence. The ministry experience should be fun. Those praying on teams for the young have been mentored and should have no criminal record.

Responsibilities of the child's ministry team leader and team

1. Provide a loving environment where the child feels completely safe.

2. Explain the process to the parent and child.

3. Ask questions to form lists for forgiveness, soul ties, word curses, and negative thought patterns. Or use the already completed children's questionnaire as a guide.

4. Read *The Little Skunk* and explain ways to make the skunk leave.

5. Lead the child through forgiveness.

6. Break unholy soul ties, word curses, and negative thought patterns.

7. Break the power of generational influences and, if necessary, lead the parent in repentance for these generational curses.

8. Lead the child to repent for doors that might be opened through lying, having an imaginary playmate, watching certain television shows, playing certain games, and the like. Break their influence.

9. Help the child understand the necessary changes in behavior in order to keep the skunks from returning.

10. Teach ways to change behavior, such as how to control anger, stop lying, or stop watching certain television shows.

11. Be funny if it helps.

12. Inviting the younger child to sit in your lap while you are ministering to her is a productive way to help the process.

13. Lovingly instruct the parent about issues that could reopen unwanted spiritual doors; for example, yelling at the child out of anger or allowing demonic forms of entertainment back into the home.

14. Explain how to spiritually cleanse the home of all items that can be an open door to the demonic.

15. Instruct the parent and child how to walk out and
maintain the freedom.

The process

The ministry team process will be similar to when ministering to
the child in the home. However, there will be a group that consists of
the team leader and usually two other team members. The same prayer
used in ministering deliverance at home can also be used in a team
setting. The team should always back the team leader. There should
never be any disagreement or questioning of the team leader or other
team members during a session. Unity is important, and everyone must
work well together—no competition. One word of wisdom I strongly
suggest is to always stay sensitive to the leading of the Holy Spirit. He
might direct you to pray something different. Allow Him to guide you.
The following are a few more words of direction and wisdom.

Great wisdom needs to be used when discussing issues. Do not say
anything that will make the child feel confused, rejected, or scared. If
you need to discuss topics like the child's conception through rape, the
child was not the desired sex of the parents, or that a spell was put on
the child at birth, address these questions privately to the parent. Then
pray through it in the deliverance setting. Pray something similar to
this:

Lord, I thank You that [child's name] *is a wonderful creation.
You make no mistakes. It is Your desire that* [child's name]
*is free from everything that makes him/her feel stinky like the
little skunk. We bind and break all rejection and all hurtful,
mad, and mean actions and a victim spirit that have influenced
his/her life even from the moment of his/her conception. We
bind and break the power of anger, violence, perversion, and
all trauma and abuse that have kept* [child's name] *from
complete joy and freedom. Your power and assignments are
canceled null and void. We command you to loose* [child's
name] *and go now in Jesus's name.*

Do you see how everything is prayed through in a way that will not cause alarm and further trauma? Ministry teams and parents need to use wisdom with words when ministering to the next generation. In closing, invite the overflowing presence of the Holy Spirit and seal the work by the blood of the Lamb.

~ Ministering to teens

If the questionnaire for teenagers from the resource tab of our ministry website has been completed, it should already have been read through before the session. Also, the separate questionnaire for parents of teens will also need to be completed and read through before the ministry time.

It is best for the parents not to be present in the room when ministering to teens because teens will open up and share more freely. However, I do speak with the parents on the phone and before the sessions. Their input is invaluable to how the ministry will occur. This will show where the teen and parent are in agreement, and it will also show where there are conflicts. We do not disclose everything the teen shares with us in the session to the parents. Teens need to have the understanding that they can safely share without their secrets being exposed.

After taking the teen through deliverance, if there are issues between them and their parents, we visit with both the parent and teen together about the problem. We try to help them in understanding each other's point of view and come to a godly resolution. One of the main focuses should be to help strengthen the family relationship. We try to aid in building healthy communication between the parents and teen and strategies for an open relationship. We share ideas on how they can grow and gain one another's respect.

Teens know when people are being real or fake. The first ministry session you have needs to go smoothly. This is a strategic time to win their respect and trust. If not, they will more than likely refuse to come back for further ministry. I am not advising that you allow the teen to control you or the ministry time—absolutely not. If the teen is disrespectful, mocking the team and showing no desire to be there, then shut the session down. Teens who are being forced by their parents to go through deliverance ministry and have no desire to be involved will not get freedom. The choice to engage and be committed to the process is necessary.

Here are some traits for those who work best with teens:

1. Must be patient

2. Have an easygoing personality

3. Does not always have to be right all the time

4. Easy to talk with

5. Does not give long and tiring lectures; this will shut down a teen

6. Must have a good understanding of and ability to bond with teens

7. Must be authentic

8. Willing to laugh at oneself if saying something quirky and out of date

9. Must be accepting and nonjudgmental

10. Must be able to minister on the teen's level

11. Must be transparent when necessary about their own personal testimony in overcoming strongholds. When led by the Lord, I testify how I overcame depression, how I battled bulimia for a very brief time, and how I was set free from fear and rebellion. When teens understand you have walked where many of them have walked, they are ready to receive from you. There is power in the testimony. With teens this transparency can build faith and relationship.

12. Must not be afraid to directly confront behavior

Walking out the freedom
Once freedom has come, it is necessary to teach them how to walk it out and maintain it.

Pray for cleansing of the child's room and the home
The child's room will be freed and cleansed of every dark spirit that was exposed and dealt with in the session. Get rid of every game, toy, picture, gift, poster, comic book, book, music, video, and so on that added to or opened the door to the demonic oppression. Invite the Lord's presence into the room. It is time to house clean—the entire home. Ask the Holy Spirit to guide you in what needs to be thrown out to pave the way for a free and healthy spiritual environment.

Deal with habits
Demonic influence affects behavior and habits. It may take time for established bad habits to come to a final stop. Instruct the parents to speak encouragement and the new kingdom identities, as these are positive influences in the recovery process. Depending on the behavior, reinforce to the parents that consistent consequences may be needed to break habits. Advise them to speak the kingdom identities during the night hours while the child is sleeping.

Advice to Parents After the Deliverance Session

~ Keep open communication lines
All children, especially teenagers, need to talk. If the parents are too busy, then other admired and trusted peers will become the confidant. It is during these years of maturing where many opinions concerning life, values, religious beliefs, and political beliefs are formed. Wise parents will converse and provide information to help the child make good choices. I have prayed for many children who fell into sin and rebellion due to the void of not having wise counsel in the home. Siblings and peers became the guiding voice, and many times the results have been negative.

After deliverance, your child might want to talk and will need a sympathetic ear. Teenagers need mothers and fathers who make themselves available and are willing to listen. It helps them in clarifying thoughts, releases emotional pressures, and makes them open to receive advice at the right time. Discerning parents will recognize the signs and will be ready to listen, discuss, and advise as needed.

~ Set aside time for family worship and prayer

There is no better way to unite a family than by giving God first place. The timing will need to be determined with careful consideration. Pick one day of the week and a specific time that works into the family's routine, and worship, pray, and read God's Word together.

> Write these commandments that I've given you today on your hearts. Get them inside of you and then get them inside your children. Talk about them wherever you are, sitting at home or walking in the street; talk about them from the time you get up in the morning to when you fall into bed at night. Tie them on your hands and foreheads as a reminder; inscribe them on the doorposts of your homes and on your city gates.
>
> —Deuteronomy 6:6–9, The Message

This time does not need to be a religious type of setting but a fun, family time. Sometimes there is one parent who does not see the need or want to do this, but do not let this stop the rest of the family. Make time to enjoy the presence of God together as a unit.

~ Engage in spiritual warfare prayer

While in the midst of writing this chapter, I received a phone call from a friend. She and her husband are foster parents. We have proof that the birth mother of the baby placed in their home is involved in witchcraft. She openly admitted that she casts spells. This precious nine-month-old baby had a required visit with his birth mother twenty-four hours before our phone conversation.

As we spoke, the baby was fussing in the background. Discerning his distressed cry, I asked, "Is he OK?" My friend, understandably concerned, shared that he had been disturbed and crying since the visit. Without hesitation, we prayed over the phone, "We break all

witchcraft curses and the fear and anxiety this birth mother released
over this precious baby. We say every curse, hex, vex, and act of
divination spoken over this child by his birth mother is canceled, null
and void by the authority of Jesus. All resulting fear and anxiety, we
break your power and say, 'Go now!' Lord, we ask for Your peace, love,
joy, and comfort to wash over him from the top of his head to the soles
of his feet."

Instantly that precious baby went from crying to joyful laughter.
We cannot be shy to engage in warfare over our young. It is time to
open our mouths and, in faith, war when directed by God.

> *Father, we rejoice in the newfound freedom our children and
> we are walking in. We are so grateful that You desire each
> of us to be more than conquerors in Christ. There has never
> been the slightest doubt in our minds that You who started this
> great work in us would keep at it and bring it to a flourishing
> finish on the very day Christ Jesus appears (Phil. 1:6). And we
> say that we will bless the Lord who guides us; even at night our
> hearts instructs us. We know the Lord is always with us. We
> will not be shaken, for He is right beside us. No wonder our
> hearts are glad, and we rejoice. Our bodies rest in safety (Ps.
> 16:7–9). You have turned our mourning into joyful dancing.
> You have taken away our clothes of mourning and clothed us
> with joy that we might sing praises to You and not be silent. O
> Lord, my God, we will give You thanks forever (Ps. 30:11–12).*

Chapter 11

Out of the Mouth of Babes
Comes Spiritual Authority

K ENDALL WAS FOUR years old. I was cooking dinner and suggested that she clean her room. Being an obedient child, she happily agreed. Shortly she returned to the kitchen and stood with her hands on her hips, tapping her foot as if she was mad.

"Momma, you want to know what just happened?"

"Sure, baby. What?"

"Momma, you told me to clean my room. Well, there was one of those little bad things. You know, Momma, those bad things in my room."

"Honey, do you mean a demon?" Let me interject before continuing that we did not talk about demons and darkness around our young children, because we did not want to frighten them. But our oldest daughter has always been sensitive to the spirit realm and, as was discussed in chapter 2, began seeing in the spirit realm at a very young age.

"Yes, Momma, that bad thing. You know what it said to me?"

Not liking the thought that a demon was in my baby's room, I quickly replied, "Yes, baby. I do want to know what it said."

Tapping her foot quicker and harder, she said, "Well, it told me not to clean my room!"

Having my complete attention, I asked her what she did.

Smiling in pleasure, she replied, "I stomped on its head and told it no in Jesus's name! And you know what, Momma? It disappeared! And you want to know something else, Momma?"

Totally intrigued, I responded, "Yes, baby. I do want to know something else."

With total confidence in her wisdom and understanding, she began

169

to teach me. "Momma, we all have angels. You have angel, Daddy has angel, and the babies have angels. And, Momma, the angels help us. They have that pointy, shiny thing, Momma. You know the thing they hold that is shiny."

"Do you mean a sword?"

"Yes, Momma, that! You know what, Momma? They take that sword and do this!" I observed as my four-year-old daughter acted out an angel using a sword as if in a spiritual battle. "And Momma, when the angels do that, the demons disappear! Momma, you want to know something else?"

Wondering what else would flow out of that baby's mouth, I replied, "Yes, I do!"

"Momma, those demons do not like you and Daddy. No, not at all! You know what they do when you pray in Jesus's name?"

"No, baby. What do they do?"

"Well, Momma, they do this." Enacting her story, my daughter began to aggressively shake her body as if nervous and in a loud voice exclaimed, "'AAAAAGGGGHHHHHH!!!!' And then they disappear! Momma, those demons don't like you and Daddy. No, not at all!"

My daughter happily left the kitchen to return to cleaning her room. Amazed, I called my husband and explained that I just had a spiritual warfare 101 lesson conducted by our four-year-old!

No Junior Holy Spirit

It does not take long when you work with the young to realize that there is not a junior Holy Spirit. The Lord does use our young, and in incredible, supernatural ways. Let's look at three scriptural examples.

~ King Josiah

What took place in Josiah's life was astounding to everyone but God. It is written in 2 Kings 22:2 that King Josiah did what was right in the Lord's sight. He sought after the presence of God. The first thing he did when he turned eighteen was go to the temple and order repairs done on the broken-down building. For years the leaders and the people worshiped pagan gods, pushing aside the Lord and the temple. Many people believed that they would never return to Yahweh worship, and even more had left God entirely. The most comfortable response for Josiah would have been to keep the status quo, but he acknowledged that there was something special about that old building.

While the carpenters were busy reworking the temple, the high priest Hilkiah discovered something exceptional. He dusted off a great book that used to be studied and venerated. It detailed the laws given to Israel by God. Hilkiah gave the book to the scribe who served King Josiah. He took the book and read it before the king.

Josiah had never before heard God's Word. He certainly had not heard those accounts through his father or grandfather. Those stories had been virtually forgotten. But rather than passing off the laws of God as antiquated and out of touch with the present world, Josiah was deeply and profoundly influenced. He tore his clothes as a sign of deep mourning that he and his kingdom had lost God's Word.

His whole society had been living without God, primarily because of the sins of his father and grandfather. Was Josiah going to do the same thing his family had done in perpetuating this sin? Was he going to cave in and reign with a bloody fist and serve idols?

I think that what was most tempting in Josiah's life was to buckle under the expectations of everyone close to him and be the egocentric, cruel monarch that was his legacy. Josiah made a conscious decision that his life would stand for more. He would follow God, in spite of who his father was. Josiah ordered that the words of the book of the Lord would be obeyed. Those pagan gods would not be appeased while he was king. Not only did Josiah read the book, but he also had it read to all of the inhabitants of Israel so that they would recognize what choice they had before them, that they were not slaves to the works their fathers and mothers did before them.

Josiah stood by the pillar of the temple and established a covenant to follow God. He had all of the pagan material that had desecrated it for so long brought out and burned. If the idols were destroyed, Josiah knew that those specific ones would never return. He then fired all of the idolatrous priests that his father had employed. Some were put to death on the altars where they themselves had sacrificed infants. Josiah dismantled every pagan altar and idol in the territory that offended God. He stopped the practice of child sacrifice to the dark god Molech. Josiah destroyed everything wicked. Nothing corrupt was to stay in Judah.

> And like unto him was there no king before him, that turned to the Lord with all his heart, and with all his soul, and with all his might, according to all the law of Moses.
>
> —2 Kings 23:25, kjv

Judah was blessed during the reign of Josiah. He turned the tide of evil that his fathers had constituted and lived a life of integrity and honor. Why does this old story sound so familiar? Countless youth and believers come from far less than perfect lines of fathers. They frequently question their worth because their fathers or mothers were alcoholic, abusive, workaholics, atheists, or not even there at all. Many have parents and relatives who look down on them and write them off, believing the lie that they will turn out worthless like their fathers or mothers. Many accept the pain of their parents' curse. We don't have to live like this. I believe that God elaborated on the story of King Josiah so that we would know that we are not trapped in family patterns and have the free will to be a new creation.

What's more, our youth can do it with passion and boldness. Just like Josiah, doing away with the pagan priests and idols worshiped by his fathers, they can level the pagan altars built by past generations such as sin, traumatic circumstances, or rebellion. They can choose to be clean of it! We can help them. There is the choice, by an absolute act of will, to be set free. Just as witnessed in Josiah's life, we can see the authority in our young released, empowering them to be great lovers of God, kingdom influencers, history makers, leaders, and role models.

~ King David

Prior to becoming king, David achieved a great triumph over the Philistine enemies during the time of King Saul. At age seventeen, he was called by King Saul to the battlefield to play music for him.

Meanwhile the giant Philistine Goliath taunted the Israelites and challenged them to send out their strongest soldier to do a one-on-one battle to prove which side was the strongest. Goliath, being around ten feet tall, had no doubts he would win.

When David heard Goliath cursing the God of Israel, he inquired, "What shall be done for the man who kills this Philistine and takes away the reproach from Israel? For who is this uncircumcised Philistine, that he should defy the armies of the living God?" (1 Sam. 17:26, NKJV).

Though he had never been a soldier, David was appalled to hear Goliath's insults. And the inactivity of the Israelites motivated him to do something. He approached Saul and told how he had killed a lion and a bear that had endangered his family's sheep (v. 36).

Saul offered David his armor, but it was too big and heavy. So he went out to battle with his sling, some pebbles, and his staff. When Goliath saw how small young David was, he mocked him, saying "Am I a dog, that you come to me with sticks?…Come to me, and I will give your flesh to the birds of the air and the beasts of the field!" (vv. 43–44, NKJV).

David's response: "You come to me with a sword, with a spear, and with a javelin. But I come to you in the name of the LORD of hosts, the God of the armies of Israel, whom you have defied. This day the LORD will deliver you into my hand, and I will strike you and take your head from you. And this day I will give the carcasses of the camp of the Philistines to the birds of the air and the wild beasts of the earth, that all the earth may know that there is a God in Israel" (vv. 45–46, NKJV).

David rushed forward, took a stone out of his bag, and slung it at Goliath. It struck the giant's forehead, and he fell over. David then took Goliath's sword and cut off his head. The shocked Philistines then fled as the Israelites routed them. Friends, a seventeen-year-old boy had the boldness to battle and kill a giant that no other Israelite would fight. There is authority in our young.

~ Jesus

Being obedient to the Law, Mary and Joseph returned to Nazareth, which would be Jesus's home until He started His ministry. What did He do during the hidden years at Nazareth? Luke reports that he developed physically, mentally, socially, and spiritually.

Jesus did not perform any miracles as a boy. He worked with Joseph in the carpenter shop (Matt. 13:55; Mark 6:3) and apparently ran the business after Joseph died. Joseph and Mary had other children during those years. Jesus was part of a family.

Luke gives us only one story from Jesus's youthful years. Joseph and Mary were devout Jews who observed Passover in Jerusalem. Three times a year the Jewish men were required to go to Jerusalem to worship, but not all of them could afford the journey. If they chose one feast, it was usually the Passover; they tried to take their family because it was the most important feast on the Jewish calendar.

People traveled to the feasts in caravans. Relatives and whole villages often traveled together and kept an eye on each other's children. At the age of twelve, Jesus could easily have gone from one group to another and not been missed. Joseph would think Jesus was with Mary and the other children, while Mary would suppose He was with Joseph and the men.

They had gone a day's journey from Jerusalem when they discovered that Jesus was missing. It took a day to return to the city and another day to find Him. During those three days, Joseph and Mary had been greatly distressed (Luke 2:48). Being a parent, I can imagine the intensity of their concern. Three days is an agonizingly long time to lose your child.

Whether Jesus had spent the entire time in the temple, we don't know. We do know that when Joseph and Mary found Him, He was in the midst of the teachers, asking them questions and listening to their answers. The teachers were amazed at both His questions and answers.

Can you imagine Mary and Joseph's relief when they first saw Jesus from a distance? Mary's loving rebuke brought a respectful but astonished reply from Jesus: "Why is it that you were looking for Me?

Did you not know that I *had to be* in My Father's house?" (Luke 2:49, NAS, emphasis added). Jesus was affirming His divine sonship and mission to do the will of the Father. Jesus often used the word *must*: "I must preach" (Luke 4:43); "The Son of man must suffer" (Luke 9:22); the Son of man "must be lifted up" (John 3:14). Even at the age of twelve, Jesus was moved by a divine urge to do the Father's will. Just as Jesus was maturing physically, His calling, authority, and anointing were increasing in preparations of His earthly ministry.

Since Jesus increased in wisdom, we wonder how much He understood God's divine plan at that time. Certainly He grew in His understanding of those mysteries as He communed with His Father and was taught by the Spirit. One thing was sure. Joseph and Mary didn't fully understand! And I have no doubt that these types of occurrences happened again as Jesus matured. I believe we too can partner with God in preparing our young in the ways of the Lord as they grow.

Jesus is a wonderful role model for all young people. He grew in a balanced way without neglecting any part of life. All the while, His priority was to do the will of His Father. He knew how to listen and ask the right questions. He learned how to work and was obedient to His parents.

The boy Jesus grew up in a large family, in a despised city, nurtured by parents. The Jewish religion was at an all-time low, the Roman government was in control, and society was in a state of fear. Yet when Jesus emerged from Nazareth eighteen years later, the Father was able to say of Him, "You are My Son, My Beloved! In You I am well pleased" (Luke 3:22, AMP). May we learn how to raise our young to the fullness of all God is calling them to!

Justice Contends for Freedom at Grandma's House

The following story is a powerful example of another four-year-old's gift of discernment in operation written by my friend Kim Johnson.

One afternoon my grandsons were visiting. Suddenly,
Justice, in his discerning four-year-old manner, states,
"Nana, there's a monster over there!"

I immediately asked him, "What does he look like?"

"He's got a big black head!"

"Really. What is his name?" "His name is T-R-I."

I was amazed that this child who cannot write his name
yet replied by spelling the monster's name. I questioned
him again.

He said, "Yes, Nana. It's T-R-I."

"Well, Justice. Do you want Nana to pray and ask Jesus
to send angels in to lasso him up and take him away?"

"Yeah!" he replied with a glimmer in his eyes.

As I began to pray, Justice watched enthusiastically,
smiled, and nodded his head in agreement when I finished
the prayer. "Is he gone, Justice?"

"Yup," he replied.

A few minutes later he walked into the next room,
stepped into the walk-in closet, and told me, "Nana, there's
a monster in here."

"What's his name?"

"L-A-N."

"Justice, this time I want you to pray, and Nana will
stand in agreement with you. OK?"

He nodded yes, and with authority he stepped up onto
a footstool, pointed his finger at the monster, and sternly
declared: "Jesus says, 'GET OUT!'" Completely satisfied,
he stepped down off the stool and confidently told me that
L-A-N was gone.

That same weekend, my husband's daughter kept
calling wanting to get a tiger's eye statue that my husband
was keeping for her. So much time had passed we had
forgotten about it. He wasn't sure where it was and took
some time finding it after her persistent attempts to
retrieve it. When he pulled it out, it was a big, black tribal

head that stood all of four inches tall! It was exactly what Justice described when he saw TRI and LAN. It was as if this demonic object could no longer stay since Justice and I prayed.

We Cannot Trap Our Young by Religious Spirits

What if my friend had ignored Justice and said, "What you are seeing is only your imagination"? I shared in the introduction that statistics say that only 4 percent of this younger generation will be evangelical Christians. Could it be that not only is the battle raging against them in the world and through the enemy, but also that we stifle them in our religious ways of putting God in a box?

This younger generation can spot authentic freedom quickly. They can discern a religious spirit in operation from a mile away. They will not be fooled. It is time to get things real and free. Do we embrace them in church, or do we judge them?

What is a religious spirit? It is a demonic force that influences people to act pious, self-righteous, or superspiritual. It avoids true spiritual authority, denies the power and gifts of God, and lives by rules and legalism instead of relationship with the Lord. It does things the way they have always been done. It disorients one's perception of who Jesus is, and it stands in the way of God's efforts to build His glorious church. It resists change and causes critical, judgmental thinking.

The reality is, our youth are bored and see no life in church or in Christianity. I realize there are wonderful parents and churches making a great impact on the next generation, but I will state fairly confidently that many are not offering deliverance ministry for their young or their families. Empowering our youth does not come from incredible light shows, technology, and media. While I am a believer in allowing all of this, if there are no power, kingdom authority, love, anointing, true relationship, interest, and a fathering and mothering heart of mentoring behind it, what purpose does this serve? If there is no experiencing of the Spirit but only rules, dead religion, and legalism, our youth will look to the world and other supernatural means to fill this void. Based on the information already discussed, most of the time they will look in wrong places, and the enemy will aggressively take advantage of the church's or parents' lack of modeling.

When we were associate pastors in Houston, one thing that was instrumental for our young was allowing them to experience God. They prayed and prayer-walked neighborhoods with us. We allowed them to conduct church services where they led worship and taught the adults. They participated in altar ministry times for those needing prayer.

Children and youth love to get out on the streets and impact a neighborhood, witness to the lost, and see firsthand people being healed. They have authority and anointing flowing through them. Do they have to grow and mature? The answer is yes. But for the most part, we have had our children stuck in programs instead of teaching and allowing them to experience and flow in the anointing of the Holy Spirit. Do we value their input? Do we listen to the prophetic dreams God gives them and teach them through this?

How Do We Teach Authority?

Now is the time to bring freedom and instruct our young in their kingdom identity and authority.

+ When our children say they are seeing in the spirit realm, believe them and teach and instruct them through this.

+ Worship and pray together.

+ Teach them God's Word.

+ Allow them to be at the altar while ministry is occurring to witness people getting saved, set free, and healed.

+ When they receive prophetic revelation from God, allow them to talk about it and help them process this.

+ Do not disregard what they are seeing or hearing because of their young age.

- Teach them how to lay hands on people and to minister.

- Encourage them to be bold in their faith.

- Give them opportunity to use their gifts.

- Let them pray aloud in the church prayer meetings.

- Be aware that there is not a junior Holy Spirit, so do not treat your children as if this is true.

- Do not judge the youth.

- Build true and honest relationships with them.

- Do not treat them as an afterthought.

- Do not glorify the darkness by focusing on and talking about it all the time.

- Pray and ask God to release the anointing, gifting, and authority in your children.

We were in a transition time. During this season the region the Lord was calling us to was a large focus of prayer for our family. Kendall had three dreams showing the next place we were to live would have mountains covered in snow. My husband was offered an associate pastor's position in a town by the name of Pampa, Texas. Folks, this place is flat. You can see for miles. There are no trees and not even a hint of one rolling hill, just Texas tumbleweeds tumbling along in the breeze. I mean that literally.

Having been unanimously voted in by the church leadership team, we were going to say yes. I will never forget the nine-year-old voice from the backseat of our minivan. "But Daddy, Jesus told me that there would be snow and mountains in the next place we live. Where are the snow and mountains, Daddy? I don't see them."

Greg and I knew to take this to heart, pray, and listen. A week later we called and turned down this pastorate position in belief that the next place we would live would have snow and mountains. Within a month we had a job offer to move to Colorado Springs, Colorado, and to work with Peter and Doris Wagner at Wagner Leadership Institute and Global Harvest Ministries. Trust me, there are a lot of mountains and more than enough snow! Out of the mouth of babes, the Lord does speak.

Lord, thank You for the blessing of our children. We know that You have greatly and uniquely gifted them. Teach us to know and discern their gifting and to give them the freedom to flow in Your anointing. We welcome Your guidance. We speak a release of the anointing and authority in their lives. We say that there is freedom of the Lord in our home and in our youth. Holy Spirit, give them dreams, visions, prophetic revelations, prayer burdens, a heart for the lost, an authority to stand, and an understanding of the truth of who they are in You. Give them a passion to seek after You and to stand on Your truths and Word. Give us the wisdom on how to encourage, release, and bless Your plans and purposes in their lives. Help us not to be religious but free in You. Give us the ability to impart this freedom and authority to the next generation. Thank You, Lord. Amen.

Chapter 12

Turning the Hearts of the Fathers to the Children and the Hearts of the Children to the Fathers

LEE IS AN anointed man of God being raised in his nation of Korea to be a spiritual father to the next generation. He is one of the most passionate prayer warriors I have ever met. As Lee shared his testimony, it was difficult to hold back the tears.

Lee literally is a walking miracle. He was raised in a home by an abusive father—a lot of physical, mental, and emotional abuse. Due to this impossible living situation, Lee became extremely depressed and began cutting himself. His depression soon turned to despair. The cutting soon led to suicidal thoughts. He was desperate to escape the abuse and wanted to end his young, tormented, fatherless life. He attempted suicide seven times—several times by hanging himself. Each time the noose broke. Several times he made overdose attempts. However, the drugs did not end his life. There was no medical explanation as to why the drugs did not kill him, but miraculously they did not.

At the age of eighteen, he was radically saved. The Lord did a deep healing work in Lee's heart. Transformed by the love of our heavenly Father, Lee chose to forgive his earthly father and to pray for his salvation. Where there was hurt and betrayal, Lee honestly felt complete forgiveness and an unhindered love for his abusive father. In time, Lee's father repented and became a Christian. He now attends the church that young Lee is pastoring. Lee's father is a taxi driver. The Lord has done such a deep work in him that many times he is overcome by the presence of God, and he weeps as he drives. Where he was once a hard man, he is now free and experiencing the Father's heart. Listen to the beautiful words this once abusive father shares with his son: "Lee, I might be your physical father, but you are now my spiritual father." Friends, no wound is too deep for our God to heal.

Getting the People Ready for God

> He'll be filled with the Holy Spirit from the moment he leaves his mother's womb. He will turn many sons and daughters of Israel back to their God. He will herald God's arrival in the style and strength of Elijah, soften the hearts of parents to children, and kindle devout understanding among hardened skeptics—he'll get the people ready for God.
>
> —Luke 1:15–17, The Message

When John the Baptist was born, his father prophesied that he was destined to *turn the hearts of the fathers to the children* (Luke 1:17). He was the forerunner, preparing the way for God to move. All of us long for revival. We desire it at a personal, family, and corporate level.

This rising generation is living in the most strategic time in the history of the church. We are living in a day and time where the love of the mothers and fathers to their children and the love of spiritual mothers and fathers to their spiritual children are crucial. One of the main focuses in the coming move of God will be the literal turning and returning of the fathers and mothers to the children and the children to the mothers and fathers. The above story shares how an entire family can be turned to one another and God. However, I know the reality is that many of you reading this book have prodigals who have wandered from home, love, and a personal relationship with God.

Prodigals Return!

This story in Luke 15:11–32 is called the Parable of the Prodigal Son. The word *prodigal* means "wasteful." But I believe a more fitting title is the Parable of the Loving Father, because it stresses the graciousness of the father more than the sinfulness of the son. It was the memory of his father's goodness that brought the boy to repentance and forgiveness. I want to reiterate again: it is time for the Father's heart to touch a fatherless generation, a time of restoration to the hearts of the mothers and fathers to their children and the children to the mothers and fathers. Let's look at the three experiences of the son.

~ Rebellion

According to Jewish law, an elder son received twice as much as the other sons. A father could distribute his riches during his lifetime if he wished. It was absolutely legal for the younger son to ask for his portion of the estate and even to sell it, but it was certainly not a loving act. It was as if he were saying to his father, "I wish you were dead!" Oftentimes our worst difficulties begin when we are able to do just as we please.

We are always heading for trouble if we treasure things more than people, pleasure more than responsibility, and distant scenes more than the blessings we have right at home. Jesus once warned two quarreling brothers, "Listen and beware of covetousness!" (See Luke 12:15.) The covetous person can never be satisfied, no matter how much he gains. A dissatisfied heart leads to a frustrated life. The prodigal learned the hard way that you cannot enjoy the things money can buy if you dismiss the things money cannot buy.

The distant country he left for is not necessarily a remote place to travel to, because it exists in our hearts. The younger son dreamed of enjoying his freedom far from home, away from his father and older brother. He needed to have his own way, so he rebelled against his own father and broke his heart.

But life in the distant country was not what he expected. His resources ran out, his friends left him, a famine came, and the son was forced to do for a stranger what he would not do for his father. He had to go to work! Sin promises freedom but brings slavery. It promises success but brings failure. It promises life, but as God's Word so distinctly shares, "the wages of sin is death" (Rom. 6:23). The boy embraced the lies of rebellion and thought he would discover himself, but he lost himself! When God is removed from our lives, enjoyment becomes captivity.

~ Repentance

To repent means to change one's mind. That is precisely what the young man did as he took care of the pigs. Eventually he came to himself, which indicates that up to this point he had not really been himself. Warren Wiersbe shares the powerful revelation that there is an insanity in sin that appears to paralyze the image of God within us and liberate the animal inside.[1]

The young man changed his mind about himself and his position and acknowledged that he was a sinner. He professed that his father was generous and that service at home was far better than freedom in the distant country. It is God's goodness, not just man's badness, that draws us to repentance. If the boy had considered only his hunger and homesickness, then he would have despaired. But his dreadful circumstances helped him to see his father in a new way, which brought hope: if his father was so honorable to servants, maybe he would forgive a son.

Had he stopped there, the boy would have felt only sorrow, but honest repentance affects the will as well as the mind and the emotions. He said, "I will rise up...I will go...I will say..." Resolutions may be worthy, but unless we pursue them and take action, they can never effectuate any permanent good. If repentance is genuinely the work of God, the sinner will obey God and put saving faith in Jesus.

~ Restoration and rejoicing

The father not only raced to welcome his son back, but he also celebrated the boy's return by preparing a great banquet. The father never allowed the younger son to finish his confession. He interrupted him, forgave him, and ordered the celebrating to begin!

The father in this story exemplifies the attitude of our heavenly Father toward repentant hearts. He is deep in His mercy and grace and outstanding in His love. Because of the sacrifice of Jesus on the cross, we are saved by God's grace, a love that pays a price.

In the East, older men do not run, yet the father ran to receive his son. One obvious reason was his endless love for him. But something else is involved. This boy had brought disgrace to his family and village.

According to Deuteronomy 21:18–21, he should have been stoned to death. If the neighbors had started casting stones, they would have struck the father who was embracing him! What a depiction of what Jesus did for us on the cross!

Everything the younger son had desired to encounter in the distant place, he discovered back home: clothes, jewelry, friends, joyful festivity, love, and confidence for the future. What had changed? Rather than saying, "Father, give me!," he said, "Father, make me!" He was willing to serve! The father did not expect him to earn his forgiveness, because good works cannot save us from our sins. In the distant country the prodigal learned the significance of misery. But back home he discovered the substance of mercy.

The ring was a mark of sonship, and the "best robe" was validation of his family's acceptance. You see, servants did not wear rings, shoes, or expensive garments. The banquet was the father's means of expressing his delight and sharing it with others. Had the son been dealt with according to the law, there would have been a funeral, not a feast.

I know there are many reading this book whose young have wandered in rebellion, lost their way, and are trapped in that distant land. But be encouraged and strengthened this day. The promising word of the Lord is that we are in a day where God is moving and restoring the relationship between the fathers and sons, mothers and daughters, and parent and child. It is a time of rejoicing in His goodness.

A Modern-Day Prodigal Returns

I asked a special young woman whom I love dearly to share her personal testimony. For some, freedom comes through a deliverance session. For others, it comes through worship, prayer, and reading the Word. But for my sweet friend, freedom came from a prayer prayed from a desperate and surrendered heart in a cold, dark prison cell. Friends, let this be an encouragement to you that God does deliver out of the worst circumstances, that remote distant country, and brings complete repentance, freedom, restoration, and rejoicing.

My father was a minister. He'd been a Christian recording artist, author, traveling evangelist, and pastor. His life's focus was on how he could benefit others.

When I was three years old, I remember watching the construction crew pour the cement foundation for our first church building. Dad would drop by to bring drinks for the workmen and check on them every few days; he would often take me with him.

To me, our church was beautiful. Anytime the doors were open, we were there. I loved going to church. Everyone knew and loved me. I loved to show off in my pretty outfits. With my curly blonde hair and big brown eyes, I just knew I was the center of everyone's attention. We were all very close regardless of our age, race, or gender. We were a happy family in Christ.

Mom was a popular Sunday school teacher, directed the children's choir, and produced musicals. She always included fun games, art projects, and brought cool snacks. We enjoyed her playful approach. Whether a child could sing or not, she'd be certain they would play a special part.

In elementary school, it seemed life was perfect. I attended a private school and had many friends. The children who lived on our street and I would play outside until sunset. We had no interest in playing video games or watching television. We spent our time playing games of Tag and Mother May I. We didn't have a care in the world.

One day Mom and Dad sat my older brother and me down for a family talk. They explained that God was changing our family's assignment. We needed to move. It was heartbreaking, but we knew this was necessary. We moved away from the friends I'd grown up with. It was a rough adjustment, and it wasn't long before my brother went away to college and my father suddenly resigned his position on the church staff. It was as if our family was thrown into the hardest test of faith ever.

As a ten-year-old girl, going through many life changes and trying to find myself was hard. But most of all I felt lonely; I desperately wanted to fit in. It seemed as though my world was falling apart. In my desire to fit in, I looked for and found new friends. Soon I was with the cool, older crowd and felt I had made it. I was on top of the world with no worries. Before long I was caught up in the drug culture where I would spend the next eleven years chasing drugs, getting high, and running from God.

At first, I was strongly convicted. In my heart I knew what I was doing was wrong. I was selling myself short and sinning against God. I deceived my parents. I deceived myself. The more conviction I felt from God, the more drugs I took to numb my senses.

I experienced times of deep sorrow, such as when I attended the funeral of my first friend who was shot and killed before he turned twenty. I lost friends to car accidents, drug overdoses, and gang-related attacks. I faced life experiences a teenager should never encounter. In my most desperate times, I wanted to draw near to Jesus, but I felt so ashamed it seemed impossible.

I was in and out of treatment centers and moved from school to school. My parents did all they could to help me. Many people were praying for me. At times the truth about my downward spiraling lifestyle would sink in; I would struggle for freedom, but the drugs always won.

In our Baptist church we learned to save ourselves for marriage. I too accepted that commitment to the Lord and wore a promise ring. My unsaved friends didn't understand why a drug addict would be so determined to save her virginity until marriage. I became a joke among the guys, and my "friends" laughed at me behind my back.

Before long, I abandoned my commitment. To my thinking, I was already a failure, so why would my promise to God mean anything anyway? At seventeen I found myself pregnant. Sadly, my biggest concern after reading the pregnancy test was how I would stay sober long enough to carry my baby full term. I'm truly grateful to God for giving me a healthy baby boy.

Two years after my son's birth, I tried methamphetamines for the first time. I'd do any and every drug that was offered to me, but meth was different. For a while, I had no desire to try it. I saw that people who did meth couldn't sleep. Some lost their minds. Within a few short months of using this drug, my life was turned completely upside down.

I quit the job I loved and began selling drugs full-time. My son, a beautiful two-year-old, needed me, but I let him stay with his grandparents so I didn't have to deal with him. I knew he'd be lovingly cared for, and that way I could focus on my next high and not feel guilty when I saw his sweet face. Meth was different from any other drug. It wasn't a social drug. I used this drug alone, not to be cool or fit in. It consumed my life. I'd go for days without sleep and food. My every thought was set on my next high.

My friends called my mother and told her that if something didn't change, I would die. That didn't come as a shock. I'd buried plenty of friends, but for some reason I didn't care if drugs took my life. One morning, right before Christmas, my momma called. She asked me to write out my last will and testament and to make plans for my son's future. She said she felt certain she would bury me soon if something didn't change. That *should* sober any normal person, but I couldn't care less. I laughed and told her there was nothing she could do to make me stop, but deep inside I was crying. I knew I desperately needed God and a miracle.

Life as I knew it was over. I had no future goals. My eyes were hollow; my face was weathered and broken out. My skin oozed crystal-like junk that also seeped through the pores on my arms. My cheeks were deeply sunken to the bones that framed my face. I was on the brink of death. Where was the pretty little girl who would light up the room? Where was the beauty contest winner? Where was the high school salutatorian academic winner? Instead I was a shell of a person, bound and blinded by addiction.

At this time my parents began to feel the Lord directing them to pray differently. They slowed down on reminding the Lord of all my problems, and they focused on thanking Him for my protection, salvation, and freedom. As they began to be thankful for the small changes, even in the midst of all the trouble, it brought some peace to their hearts and allowed them to trust the Lord with my life. It opened their eyes to see the small changes in me. In turn, this allowed me to know every small step was worth it, and my freedom was something I could reach. It didn't seem so impossible. Their persistent newly focused prayers began to help—as did their unconditional love. Not one time did they ever fail to show me God's love. This served as my reminder that God was still there and that He would accept me back no matter what. In spite of all of this, I still had to come to the bottom, that place of desperation where I knew I had to have that rescuing miracle power of God.

One day I decided to pack my things and go to San Antonio, Texas. I thought the police were watching me; if I left, it would fix everything. The day I was set to leave I was so exhausted I lay down for a quick nap. Sometime later I was abruptly awakened by two police officers standing at the foot of my bed with guns pointing directly at me, loudly demanding me to get up and come out into the living room. I lay facedown on the floor of my apartment while three of my drug-addicted friends watched me cuffed and led to a police car. It was scary—like something you'd see in a movie.

I spent several weeks in the county jail. When Mom and Dad would bring my little boy to visit, they told him his mommy was sick, and I was. They explained to him that I couldn't come home until I was well. We would talk through a screened hole in the glass window and put our hands up to the glass and trace the outline of each other's hand. As I looked into his innocent face, I wished to God I'd made better decisions. I would have given anything to touch and hold him.

For the first few weeks all I could do was sleep. I was exhausted and malnourished, and my body was detoxing.

Gradually I began to open up and talk with the other incarcerated women. I borrowed a Bible from the girl who slept next to me and began to read the Book of Job. I read of his losses, his tormenting trial. My heart ached for Job. Job was innocent. So how could I possibly pity myself? I wanted to be strong like he was. I prayed and asked God to be with me and protect me in that awful place. I found ways to be grateful for the changes He was making in my life. I was grateful for the roof over my head, for Christ's sacrifice, the Father's forgiveness, and my second chance. You know, it's funny; no matter where you are, who you are, or what you've done, Jesus will come to you when you call upon Him.

A woman in ministry called my parents' house and said she needed to speak with them about their daughter. My dad wasn't sure if he wanted to hear what she had to say. He asked my mother to join him in their living room and then put the call on speakerphone. The lady told them her daughter had been incarcerated with me and that she had witnessed God's presence come as we prayed and studied the Word together. After my parents heard the girl's testimony, they knew the Lord was working in and through my life. This was a relief to a burden they'd carried for years.

Over the next few weeks I went to court several times, praying the judge would allow me to go to a treatment center where I could keep my baby. My family and our wonderful attorney had tried, but my release and request for treatment with my son looked slim. The night before my last court visit I called my dad and asked him how to pray. He said, "Like this: Lord, surprise us." I was surprised by his lack of words. He explained that the Lord already had a plan and He doesn't need instructions from us. The next morning a new judge was miraculously assigned to fill in for my regular judge. He instantly granted me treatment in a facility for mothers with children. Praise the Lord! He had heard and answered my prayers! Soon after I was picked up by a white van and transferred to the treatment center. There I was able to hold my son for the first time in a long while.

I may have been locked behind bars, but in the midst of it, I found a living, vital relationship with Jesus Christ that changed my life. I read Scripture every chance I got. I developed relationships and prayed with and for the other women. I felt God's presence in a jail cell full of criminals. In my head I sang worship songs as I did my chores. My heart was overwhelmed and overflowed with joy and gratitude. I wasn't free physically, but that was all right. My spirit was FREE! I was free from misery, sorrow, anger, depression, bondage, and finally free from addiction and the fear of my future.

Once I trusted God, I discovered a new me, not a perfect person but a new person. Jesus became my new best friend. Strangely, at first I couldn't cry. I was hard-hearted and didn't want to participate in the programs. But after digging deeply, dealing with myself, and letting go, I came to realize that I was capable of so much more than I'd ever known.

Our counselors encouraged us to look in the mirror

each morning and speak blessings over ourselves. That was quite hard. I didn't know myself and had little control over my life. Every time I felt pain or disappointment, I'd suppress my emotions. God helped me search my heart and deal with years of emotional pain and regret.

Finally I realized that I would have to forgive myself and let go of all that had happened, because Jesus had fully paid for my sins and God had forgiven me. Looking back now, I know God allowed me to be arrested and taken to jail to protect me from others and myself.

Do you feel stuck? Does all seem hopeless? I encourage you to forgive yourself and accept God's forgiveness. Focus on what you have, not what you've lost. Be grateful for His forgiveness, read Scripture, cry if you need to. Write in your journal. In time you'll read them and find new appreciation for the progress you've made.

We all have different stories and life experiences that have brought us to the places we are today. I'm now free from the struggles of my past. Those struggles have no power to determine my future. I've been happily married for four years. We have a loving family and a peaceful home with two sweet dogs. I've watched my "little man" learn to read, write, and play flag football. It's the simple things in life I cherish most.

Through the years I've had several opportunities to give back through counseling, acts of kindness, praying for loved ones, and so much more. God's blessed me beyond what I could ever have expected. Remember, He will be your very best friend if you let Him. Let Jesus show you, as He did me, how special you truly are to Him.

Children Are God's Best Gift

Don't you see that children are God's best gift? The fruit of the womb his generous legacy? Like a warrior's fistful of arrows are the children of a vigorous youth. Oh, how blessed are you parents, with your quivers full of children! Your enemies don't stand a chance against you; you'll sweep them right off your doorstep.

—PSALM 127:3–5, THE MESSAGE

Jesus, in our closing prayer, we want to pray in agreement with this powerful scripture and promise from Your Word. Children truly are Your best gift. We thank You for this journey You have placed us on. Give us Your complete unending love for our children and this next generation. Strengthen and anoint us to be the fathers, mothers, and leaders You have called us to be. We ask for Your supernatural guidance in this process and journey. Let us minister salvation, deliverance, love, and freedom to our young. Let us reflect Your love so freely and without compromise. Cause us to be a strong and shining reflection of Your Father's heart. May there be healing and restoration between us and our young. Where there are breaches of trust, hurt, and emotional pain, bring healing, deliverance, and restoration. We pray in agreement for the return of the prodigals. We cry in agreement, "Lord, bring them home! Touch their hearts!" We thank You for every good work You are doing that we do not even see with our physical eyes or know about, those things You are doing in their hearts to draw them to You. We thank You for that work. And for all of our children and in all areas of our lives, make us to be the loving fathers and mothers You have designed for us to be to our physical and spiritual children. Make us tenacious, passionate, and ones who do not shrink back but advance forward in Your kingdom. Let the work You have begun in our lives come to complete fruition. May Your abundant love, blessings, and heart touch us, our young, our homes, our youth groups, and our churches in deeper measure. And may Your freedom reign in all of our lives. We love You, Lord. In Jesus's name we pray, amen.

Appendix

Apparent Demonic Groupings List[1]

DEAF AND DUMB SPIRIT

Accidents
Blindness—Matt. 12:22
Burning accidents—Mark 9:22
Confusion—James 3:16
Convulsions
Crying, uncontrolled*—Matt. 15:23;
  Mark 9:26
Deafness—Ps. 38:13–14
Death—Prov. 6:16–19
Destruction—Lev. 26:21–22
Drowning accidents—Mark 9:22
Dumbness (in the Greek,
  "insanity")—Mark 9:25
Ear infection, chronic—Mark
  9:25–26
Emotionless
Epilepsy—Matt. 17:15–18
Eye diseases—Lev. 26:16
Fear of: fire—Isa. 4:4; water
Foaming at mouth—Luke 9:39;
  Mark 9:18–20
Gnashing of teeth—Mark 9:18

Infections (chronic)
Insanity
Lethargy
Lunatic behavior—Mark 9:20
Madness—Deut. 28:34; John 10:20
Motionless stupor
Pining away—Isa. 38:12; Mark 9:18
Poverty—Prov. 6:9–11
Schizophrenia
Seizures—Mark 9:18, 20, 26
Self-pity
Sensing the "approach of death"
Sleepiness—Prov. 20:13; Matt. 25:5
Stupors
Stuttering
Suicide—Mark 9:22
Tearing—Mark 9:18, 26, 29
Turrets—Job 16:9; Mark 9:18
Unbelief—Heb. 3:12
Unforgiveness—Luke 6:37
Wallowing—2 Pet. 2:22

Note: *For uncontrolled crying, also see "Spirit of Heaviness."

BIND	LOOSE
‣ Deaf and dumb spirit—Mark 9:25; Matt. 17:15	‣ Healing—Mal. 4:2; Acts 10:38 ‣ Hearing—Rom. 10:17 ‣ Boldness—Eph. 3:12

195

FAMILIAR SPIRIT
Witchcraft; Spirit of Divination

Astrology—Isa. 47:13

Automatic handwriting

Channeling

Charmer—Deut. 18:11

Charms (good luck)

Clairvoyance—1 Sam. 28:7–8

Conjuring (summoning demons to appear)—Isa. 44:25

Consulter of dead—Deut. 18:11; 1 Chron. 10:13

Cults (false religions and belief systems): Belial, Black Panthers, Buddhism, Catholicism (anything unbiblical therein), Christian Science, Confucianism, Freemasonry, Hinduism, Islam, Jehovah's Witnesses (Watchtower), KKK, mind control, Mormonism, Rosicrucianism, Satanism, Scientology, Shintoism, Taoism, theosophy, Unitarianism, unity, universalism, witchcraft

Disobedience—Rom. 1:30; Heb. 4:6

Divination—Jer. 29:8; Hosea 4:12

Doctrinal error—Lev. 19:31

Doctrinal obsession—1 Tim. 1:3–7

Dreamer (false dreams)*—Jer. 23:32; 27:9–10

Drugs

Easily persuaded

Enchanter—Deut. 18:12

False prophecies**

Family curses—Gen. 4:11

Fantasy

Fear of: God (unhealthy), hell, losing salvation

Fetishes (good-luck pieces)

Fortune-telling—Micah 5:12; Isa. 2:6; Lev. 20:6

Generational iniquity—Isa. 1:4; Matt. 27:25; John 9:1–3

Hallucinations—Rev. 21:8; 22:15

Harlotry—Lev. 20:6

Horoscope—Matt. 16:2–4; Isa. 47:13; Lev. 19:26; Jer. 10:2

Hypnosis

Idolatry—Hosea 4:12

Incantation

Incest—2 Sam. 13:14

Incubus or Succubus (unseen demon spirits)—Gen. 6:2–4

Lawlessness—1 John 3:4; 2 Thess. 1:7–8

Legalism—Gal. 1:1-7; 1 Tim. 4:1–3

Lethargy—Prov. 20:4

Levitation

Liar—1 Tim. 1:10

Magic, black/white—Exod. 7:11, 22; 8:7; Lev. 19:26

Manipulation—Titus 1:9–10

Medium—1 Sam. 28:7

Mind control—Jer. 23:16, 25, 32

Mind reading

Music that defies, mocks, or rejects God

Muttering

Necromancy (consulting the dead)—Deut. 18:11

New Age philosophies and involvement

Obsessions

Occultism—2 Chron. 33:6

Ouija board

Palmistry

Passive mind

Pendulum divination

Poverty—Prov. 6:6–11

Rebellion—1 Sam. 15:22
Religiosity—Job 15:4–6
Ritualism
Satanism
Séance
Seduction—Prov. 9:13–18
Self-will—Prov. 1:25–30
Soothsayer—Micah 5:12; Isa. 2:6;
 Jer. 27:9–10
Sorcery—Micah 5:12–15

Spirit guide(s)
Spiritism—1 Sam. 28; Lev. 20:6
Stubbornness—Lev. 26:15
Superficial spirituality—2 Tim.
 2:17–18
Suspicion
Tarot cards
Trance
Witch, witchcraft—Lev. 19:26; 20:6;
 Deut. 18:10

Consider also: conjuring, I Ching, hip-hop music, occult jewelry, martial arts, mental telepathy, horror movies, past-life readings, Pokémon, psychic healing, Reike, rock music, spiritual adultery (spiritual unfaithfulness), superstition, tea leaves, transcendental meditation, victim, voodoo, yoga

Notes: *For dreamer, also see "Lying Spirit" and "Spirit of Heaviness." **For false prophecies, also see "Lying Spirit."

BIND	LOOSE
▸ Familiar spirit, spirit of divination—Acts 16:16–18; Deut. 18:11; Lev. 20:6, 27; 1 Chron. 10:13	▸ Truth—Ps. 15:1–2; Prov. 3:3; John 8:32; 2 Cor. 13:8 ▸ Revelation—Gal. 1:12; Eph. 1:7

HAUGHTY SPIRIT (PRIDEFUL SPIRIT)

Agitated—Titus 3:3
Angry—Prov. 29:22
Argumentative
Arrogant—Jer. 48:29; Isa. 2:11, 17; 2
 Sam. 22:28
Bitter—James 3:14
Boastful—Eph. 2:8–9; 2 Tim. 3:2
Bragging—2 Pet. 2:18
Competitive, excessively
Condescending
Contentious—Prov. 13:10
Controlling
Covetous—2 Peter 2:18
Critical—Matt. 7:1
Deception—Heb. 3:12–13

Dictatorial
Domineering
Education, pride of or
 preoccupation with—Titus 3:9–11
Egocentric—Job 41:34
Egotistical
Elitist
Entitlement
False humility
Frustration
Gossip—2 Cor. 12:20
Greed—Rom. 1:29–30; 1 Tim. 6:10
Hatred—Prov. 26:26
Haughtiness—2 Pet. 2:10
Holier-than-thou attitude

Idleness
Impatience
Importance
Insolence—2 Tim. 3:3
Intellectualism—1 Tim. 1:4, 6–7
Intolerance
Irritability—Phil. 2:14
Judgmentalism—Matt. 7:1
Liar—Prov. 19:22; 1 Tim. 1:9–10
Lofty looks
Mocker—Ps. 35:16
Obstinacy—Prov. 29:1; Dan. 5:20
Overbearing
Perfectionist
Playacting
Pretension
Pride—Prov. 6:16–17; 16:18; Isa. 28:1
Rage—Prov. 6:34; Gal.5:19
Rationalism
Rebellion—1 Sam. 15:23; Prov. 29:1
Rejection of God (atheism)—1 John 2:22

Religious spirit
Resentment—Exod. 8:15
Scornful—Prov. 1:22; 3:34; 21:24
Self-centeredness—James 3:14
Self-deception—Jer. 49:16; Obad. 3
Self-delusion—Rev. 3:17
Self-importance
Selfish—Gal. 5:19
Self-pity
Self-righteousness—Isa. 64:6; Luke 18:11–12
Smug—2 Sam. 22:28; Jer. 48:29
Stiff-necked—Exod. 32:9; Acts 7:51
Stubborn—Ps. 81:11
Superiority
Theatrics
Uncompassionate
Unforgiveness—Matt. 18:35
Unkind
Vanity—Ps. 119:113; 2 Pet. 2:18
Violent—Ps. 7:16
Wrath*

Note: *For wrath, also see "Jealousy."

BIND	LOOSE
‣ Haughty/prideful spirit—Prov. 6:16–18; 16:18; 21:24; Isa. 16:6; Eccl. 7:8	‣ Humility—1 Pet. 5:5; Ps. 10:17; Prov. 22:4; 29:23 ‣ Mercy—James 2:13; 1 Pet. 2:10; Jude 2

LYING SPIRIT

Accusations—Rev. 12:10; Ps. 31:18
Adultery—2 Pet. 2:14; Prov. 6:32
Apostasy—2 Pet. 2:1–3
Arguments—2 Tim. 2:23–24
Arrogance—Isa. 2:11
Cheating
Crying—Matt. 15:23
Curses—Num. 5:24

Deceit—Ps. 101:7; 2 Thess. 2:9–13
Delusions, strong—Isa. 66:4
Depraved desires
Divination—Jer. 29:8
Doctrines, false—1 Tim. 4:1; Heb. 13:9
Dreamer
Drivenness, excessive

Drugs
Emotionalism
Exaggeration
False: burdens, compassion, doctrines, oaths (Ps. 144:8; Ezek. 21:23), prophets (Isa. 9:15), prophecy* (Jer. 23:16-17; 27:9-10), responsibility, spirituality, teaching, witness (Prov. 19:5; Matt. 15:19; Mark 10:19)
Fear of authority
Financial problems (especially with tithing)
Flattery—Prov. 26:28; 29:5
Gossip—2 Tim. 2:16; Prov. 20:19
Heresy—1 Cor. 11:19; Gal. 5:20
Homosexuality**—Rom. 1:26
Hypocrisy—Isa. 32:6; 1 Tim. 4:2
Insinuations
Jezebel spirit—Rev. 2:20; 1 Kings 18:4-13; 19:1-2
Lies—2 Chron. 18:22; Prov. 6:16-19
Lust—Ps. 81:12; Rom. 1:27
Mental bondage—Rom. 8:15; Heb. 2:15
Mind control
Passion, inordinate—Deut. 32:5
Perfectionist
Performance
Poverty—Mal. 3:8-12; Ps. 34:9-10

Pride—Prov. 6:16-17; 16:18; Isa. 28:3
Profanity
Rationalization
Religious spirit—Job 8:3-7
Robbery—Exod. 20:15; Prov. 1:10-14
Seeking of approval (insecurity)
Self-image (feel worthless, ugly, hopeless)
Self-inflicted curses—Deut. 28:15; 1 Kings 18:28
Sexual: adultery (1 Cor. 6:9-11), fantasies (Prov. 23:26-28), fornication, homosexual behavior (Rom. 1:26-27), lesbianism (Rom. 1:26-27), masturbation (Gen 38:9), pornography, sodomy***, transsexual behavior (1 Cor. 6:9), transvestite (Rom. 1:26-27)
Slander—Prov. 10:18; Rom. 12:17
Superstitions—Acts 17:22
Talking, excessive—1 Tim. 6:20
Uncleanness—Eph. 5:3-4
Vain imaginations—Deut. 29:19; Rom. 1:21; 2 Cor. 10:5
Vanity—Job 15:31
Vengeance—Rom. 12:19
Victim
Wickedness—Rom. 1:29

Notes: *For false prophecy, also see "Familiar Spirit." **For homosexuality, also see "Spirit of Perversion/Whoredom." ***For sodomy, also see "Spirit of Perversion/Whoredom."

BIND	LOOSE
‣ Lying spirit—2 Chron. 18:22; 1 Kings 22:22-23; 2 Thess. 2:7-12	‣ Honesty—1 Tim. 2:2; Prov. 16:11; Phil. 4:8 ‣ Goodness—Ps. 23:6; 2 Thess. 1:11; Eph. 5:9

SEDUCING SPIRIT

Attracted to false prophets, signs, and wonders—Jer. 14:14; Matt. 24:24

Deceived—Prov. 24:28

Easily swayed—2 Tim. 3:6

Emulation—Gal. 5:19-21

Exploitation—Prov. 9:13-18

Fascination with evil ways, evil objects, and evil persons

Fear of man

Greedy—Prov. 1:19

Gullibility

Hypocritical lies—Matt. 6:2; 1 Pet. 2:1

Music that defies, mocks, or rejects God

Seared conscience—1 Tim. 4:2

Seduced, enticed—2 Tim. 3:6; Eph. 4:4-16

Seeks attention

Sensual in dress, actions—Prov. 9:3-5

Trance

Wanders from the truth of God—2 Tim. 4:3-4

BIND	LOOSE
➤ Seducing spirit—1 Tim. 4:1; Mark 13:22; 2 Tim. 3:13	➤ Spirit of truth—John 14:17; 15:26; 1 John 4:6 ➤ Spirit of holiness—Rom. 1:4; Eph. 4:24; 1 Pet. 1:16

SHADOW OF DEATH

Abandons friends or family—1 Sam. 12:22

Aching heart

Blinded heart and mind—Acts 28:27

Deception—Isa. 8:19

Depression—Isa. 61:3

Despair—Isa. 61:1

Discouragement

Dreams of being attacked by: animals, demons, Grim Reaper

Dreams of: being chased by dead people, being flogged, being hit by a vehicle, being married to dead people, being shot, falling into a pit and being unable to get out, walking in a graveyard

Excessive mourning or grief—Isa. 61:3

Fear—2 Tim. 1:7

Hopelessness

Isolation

Lethargy

Mental torment

Murder—1 Tim. 1:9

Obsession with: blood, death (Prov. 2:17-18), violence

Oppression—Job 35:9; Prov. 3:31

Seduction—Prov. 2:16-18

Seeing shadowy, dark figure

Self-affliction—1 Kings 18:28

Sharp pains in the body—Prov. 14:30

Something keeps whispering that he or she is going to die

Sickness or disease that doesn't respond to prayers or medical treatment—Prov. 14:30

Sorrow—Isa. 35:10

Sudden loss of appetite

Suicide

Thoughts of suicide—Ps. 103:4

BIND	LOOSE
› Shadow of death—Isa. 28:15; Ps. 23:4; 44:19; 107:10–14	› Life—Rom. 8:2, 11; John 10:9–10 › Light—Dan. 5:14; Ps. 112:4; 1 John 2:8; 1 Pet. 2:9; Eph. 1:18

SPIRIT OF ANTICHRIST

Acts against the miracles of God

Acts against the Word of God—Titus 2:5

Against Christ and His teachings—2 Thess. 2:4; 1 John 4:3

Against Christians—Acts 17:13

Against God—Isa. 52:5

Attacks the saints—Acts 9:1

Attacks the testimony of Christ

Attempts to rationalize Christ

Attempts to take Christ's place

Blasphemes the Holy Spirit—Mark 3:29; Luke 12:10; 1 Tim. 1:20

Closed-mindedness

Confusion—James 3:16; 1 Cor. 14:33

Critical—Prov. 16:28

Cults*

Deceiver—1 John 2:18–26; Rom. 7:11; 2 Thess. 2:4, 10; 2 John 7

Defensiveness

Denies the atonement—1 John 4:3; 2 John 7–8

Denies the blood of Christ

Denies the deity of Christ—Matt. 26:63–64

Denies the work of the Holy Spirit

Displays open unbelief

Disturbs fellowship and gathering of the saints

Doctrinal error/twisting of doctrine—Isa. 19:14; Rom. 1:22–23; 2 Tim. 3:7–8; Acts 13:10; 2 Pet. 2:14

Explains away the miracles of God

Harasses/persecutes the saints

Humanism

Ignores and opposes Christ's blood

Judgmentalism

Lawlessness—2 Thess. 2:7

Legalism—1 Tim. 4:3

Mean-spirited—Prov. 1:19

Mocking attitude

Occult—Acts 16:16–21

Opposes: the Bible, blood of Christ, deity of Christ (1 John 4:3), doctrine of Christ (2 Tim. 3:8), fellowship of Christ, humanity of Christ, miracles, men of God (Rev. 13:7; Dan. 7:21), the ministry, victory of Christ

Persecutes the saints

Rationalizes the Word—Prov. 3:7–8

Self-exalting—2 Cor. 10:12–13; 1 Tim. 3:6

Stirs up strife between believers—1 Cor. 3:3

Suppresses ministry—Matt. 23:13

Violent—Prov. 16:29

Worldliness—1 John 4:5

Note: *For cults, also see "Familiar Spirit."

BIND	LOOSE
‣ Spirit of Antichrist—1 John 4:3; 2 Thess. 2:4	‣ Christ—Acts 15:11; 16:31; 1 Pet. 4:16; Rom. 1:16 ‣ Grace—Rom. 1:5; 6:14; Gal. 6:18; Eph. 4:7

SPIRIT OF BONDAGE

Accusation—Rev. 12:10; Col. 3:5

Addictions: alcohol, caffeine, cigarettes/nicotine, drugs (legal or illegal), food, medications (above and beyond prescribed use), sex (Ezek. 16:28–29)

Anguish of spirit—Rom. 2:9

Anorexia

Anxiety—Phil. 4:6–7

Bitterness—Eph. 4:31

Bound

Bulimia

Brokenhearted—Ps. 51:17

Bruised spirit—Ezek. 23:3

Compulsive behavior—Prov. 5:22; John 8:34

Compulsory subjection and control

Condemnation—2 Cor. 3:9

Coveting wealth in order to hoard it—Luke 12:16–21

Critical spirit—1 Pet. 2:1

Death wish—Isa. 8:19

Dominance

Doubting salvation—2 Cor. 13:5

Drivenness, excessive

Embarrassment

False burden

False compassion

False guilt

False humility—Gal. 6:3

False responsibility

Faultfinding

Fear of death—Heb. 2:14–15

Fears—Rom. 8:15

Feeling "lost"

Frustration

Gluttony—1 Cor. 6:12–13; 2 Tim. 3:3–4; Phil. 3:19

Helplessness

Hopelessness—Prov. 13:12

Hyperactivity

Inability to break free—Isa. 58:6

Idleness—Prov. 19:15

Judgmentalism—Isa. 28:6; Rom. 14:13

Lostness—Heb. 2:3

Maladies and forms of sickness: ADD/ADHD, chronic fatigue syndrome, MPD, paranoia, phantom pain (not due to loss of a limb), schizophrenia, Tourette syndrome

Medications, hooked on

Mind control

Nervousness

No assurance of salvation

Oppression—Acts 10:32
Perfectionism
Possessiveness
Poverty—Ps. 34:9–10
Rejection—Judg. 11:2–3
Resentment*
Restlessness—Isa. 28:12
Satanism—Acts 26:18
Self-condemnation—Job 9:20–21
Self-deception—Gal. 6:3
Self-pity
Self-reward (overeating, etc.)
Shame—Rev. 3:18
Slavery—Rom. 6:15–16

Spiritual blindness—2 Cor. 4:3–4
Stiffness—Acts 7:51
Strife—Gal. 5:19–20
Suicide—Matt. 27:5
Superiority
Uncontrolled spending
Unholy soul ties—Matt. 5:27–28;
    Acts 5:1–4
Unrighteousness—1 Peter 2:12
Vagabond spirit—Ps. 109:10; Acts
    19:13; 1 Tim. 5:13
Witchcraft—Nah. 3:4; Gal. 5:20
Worthlessness—Ps. 4:2

Note: *For resentment, also see "Spirit of Jealousy."

BIND	LOOSE
➤ Spirit of bondage—Rom. 8:15; Gal. 4:3; 5:1	➤ Liberty—Rom. 8:21; Gal. 5:13 ➤ Spirit of adoption—Rom. 8:15, 28

SPIRIT OF ERROR

Always right—Ps. 36:1
Angry—Prov. 29:22
Argumentative—1 Tim. 1:10
Competitive, excessively
Contentious—1 Tim. 5:13
Cults/occult—Acts 16
Defensiveness
Doctrines of devils—1 Tim. 4:1
"Easy-believism"
Error—2 Tim. 2:17–18; 1 John 4:6

False doctrines—2 Tim. 4:3
Hate—1 Pet. 2:1
Lack of discernment—Eph. 5:6
Lies—1 Tim. 4:2
New Age beliefs
Pride/haughtiness—Ps. 36:2–3
Unsubmissive—2 Tim. 3:2
Unteachable—1 Tim. 6:20–21; 2
    Tim. 3:7

BIND	LOOSE
➤ Spirit of error—1 John 4:6	➤ Spirit of truth—John 14:17; 15:26; 16:13 ➤ Spirit of promise—Eph. 1:13; Gal. 3:14

SPIRIT OF FEAR

Abandonment—Prov. 19:7
Abuse—Judg. 19:25
Accusations—Ps. 31:18
Agitation
Anxiety—1 Pet. 5:7
Apprehension
Cannot call upon God
Careful, unduly
Cautious, unduly
Compromise
Condemnation
Confusion—Jer. 3:25; James 3:16
Crying, continual—Matt. 15:23
Daydreaming
Depression—Ps. 42:5; Lam. 3:19–20
Distrust
Doubt—Matt. 8:26; Rev. 21:8
Doubting assurance of salvation
Dread—Ps. 119:39
Embarrassment—Ezra 9:6
Escapism—2 Cor. 10:4–5
Excitable, overly
Faithlessness—Prov. 14:4
Fantasy*—Gen. 6:5
Fear of: accusation, authority,
  closed-in places, condemnation,
  confrontation (Matt. 10:28),
  correction, danger (Prov. 16:4),
  darkness (Isa. 59:9–10), death (Ps.
  55:4; Heb. 2:14–15), disapproval,
  failure (Gen. 42:28), germs,
  giving/receiving love, God (in
  an unhealthy way), heights,
  judgment, losing salvation, man
  (Prov. 29:25), touching
Frustration
Hormonal imbalance
Headaches**
Heart attacks—Lev. 26:36; Ps. 55:4;
  Luke 21:26; John 14:1
High blood pressure

Hypochondria
Hysteria
Inadequacy
Indecision
Indifference
Ineptness
Inferiority complex
Insanity—Matt. 17:15
Insecurity
Insomnia
Intimidation
Isolation
Jealousy—Num. 5:14; Song of Sol.
  8:6
Judgmentalism
Lack of trust
Loneliness—Job 28:4
Low self-esteem
Mind control
Moodiness
Nightmares—Ps. 91:5–6
Negativity
No fellowship with the Father
Orphaned—Jer. 47:3
Panic
Paralysis
Paranoia
Passivity
Phobias—Isa. 13:7–8; 2 Tim. 1:7
Playacting
Pouting
Pretension
Procrastination—Prov. 6:6
Recluse
Resentment***
Restlessness
Roving
Schizophrenia—Deut. 28:28
Self-awareness, hyper- or excessive

Self-rejection
Self-reward
Sensitivity, hyper- or excessive
Sickness—2 Kings 20:1
Skepticism—2 Pet. 3:3
Sleepiness—1 Thess. 5:6–7
Sleeplessness—Prov. 4:16
Sophistication
Sorrow—Ps. 13:2; 116:3
Spiritual blindness—Isa. 56:10;
  Hosea 9:7
Stress
Stuttering—Isa. 32:4
Suspicion

Teeth-grinding—Ps. 112:10
Tension
Terror—Job 31:23
Theatrics
Timidity—2 Tim. 1:7
Torment—Ps. 55:5; 1 John 4:18
Trembling—Job 4:14; Ps. 55:5
Trust, lack of
Unbelief—Matt. 13:58; Heb. 4:11
Unreality
Unworthiness
Vexation—Eccles. 1:14
Worry—Matt. 6:25–28

Notes: *For fantasy, also see "Spirit of Whoredom." **For headaches, also see "Spirit of Infirmity." ***For resentment, also see "Spirit of Jealousy."

BIND	LOOSE
› Spirit of fear—2 Tim. 1:7; Ps. 55:5	› Peace—1 Thess. 5:23; Gal. 5:22; Eph. 4:3 › Joy—Ps. 5:11; 51:12; Gal. 5:22–23

SPIRIT OF HEAVINESS

Abandonment
Bastard (to alienate)—Deut. 23:2;
  Zech. 9:6
Brokenhearted—Ps. 69:20; Prov.
  12:18; 15:3, 13; 18:14; Luke 4:18
Burdened
Condemnation—2 Cor. 3:9
Continual sadness—Prov. 15:13;
  Neh. 2:2
Critical
Cruel—Prov. 6:34
Crying—Matt. 15:23
Death—Job 3:5; Isa. 8:19
Defeatism—Prov. 7:26–27
Despair—Job 7:15; 2 Cor. 1:8–9
Despondency—Isa. 61:3

Dejection—2 Cor. 1:8–9
Discouragement
Disgust
Disorder
Dread—Deut. 1:29
Drivenness, excessive
Escape
False burden
False guilt
Fatigue
Gloom
Gluttony
Grief—Job 6:2; Ps. 31:9
Guilt
Headache
Heartbreak, heartache

Hopelessness—2 Cor. 1:8–9
Hurt
Hyperactivity
Indifference
Inner hurts
Insomnia—Neh. 2:2
Introspection
Laziness—Prov. 19:15
Lethargy
Listlessness
Loneliness
Morbidity
Mourning, excessive—Luke 4:18;
Isa. 6:13
Pain—Jer. 6:24; 15:18; Luke 9:39
Passivity—Prov. 10:4
Poverty—Prov. 13:18
Pressure

Rejection
Restlessness—John 14:1
Self-pity—Ps. 69:20
Shame—Ps. 44:15; Eph. 5:12
Sleepiness
Sorrow—Prov. 15:13; Isa. 65:14
Suicide—Ps. 18:5
Tiredness—Isa. 40:30; 57:10
Torment—Ps. 22:16; 1 John 4:18
Troubled spirit— Luke 4:18; Prov.
18:14; 26:22
Unworthiness
Vagabond—Gen. 4:12, 14; Acts
19:13
Wanderer—Jude 13
Weariness—Ps. 109:22
Wounded spirit—Prov. 15:4; 1 Cor.
8:12

BIND	LOOSE
➤ Spirit of heaviness—Isa. 61:3; Ps. 69:20; Prov. 12:25	➤ Comforter—Heb. 13:15 ➤ Praise—Ps. 22:22; 42:11 ➤ Joy—Isa. 61:5; Neh. 12:43; Job 41:22

SPIRIT OF INFIRMITY

ADD—Matt. 8:16–17
ADHD—Mark 7:32
Allergies
Arthritis—Deut. 28:35; Prov. 14:30;
John 5:4
Asthma—John 5:4; Prov. 16:24
Bent body or spine—Luke 13:11
Bitterness—Deut. 28:20; 1 Sam. 5:6;
Job 7:11
Bleeding—Matt. 9:20
Blindness—Gen. 48:10; Lev. 26:16;
Deut. 28:28; Luke 7:21
Bronchitis
Cancer—Luke 13:11; John 5:4

Chronic diseases—Job 33:19–25; Ps.
102:5
Colds
Deafness
Death—Ps. 102:11
Diseases—Lev. 26:16
Disorders
Epilepsy—1 Sam. 21:15
Fainting—Lam. 1:13
Feebleness—Prov. 16:24
Fever—Matt. 8:15
Fungus infections—Luke 5:12
Generational curses—Exod. 20:5;
Lev. 26:39; Num. 14:18; Deut. 5:9

Hallucinations—Deut. 28:22
Hatred—Deut. 28:22
Hay fever
Headaches or migraines
Heart attack—Lev. 26:36; Ps. 102:4
Impotence—Acts 3:2; 4:9
Infections—Deut. 28:22
Inflammation—2 Chron. 21:15
Insanity—Deut. 28:28-29
Lameness—Acts 3:2; 4:9
Lunatic—Zech. 12:4
Madness—Prov. 17:22
Mania—Prov. 26:21
Mental illness—Matt. 17:15; Mark 5:5
Oppression*—Acts 10:38
Paralysis (palsy)—Ps. 102:5; Prov. 15:20; Matt. 4:24
Paranoia—Deut. 28:67

Physical disorders or trauma, lingering—Luke 13:11
Plague (curse)—Luke 7:21
Poverty—Deut. 28:20-33, 38
Schizophrenia—Deut. 28:28-29
Seizures
Senility
Skin disorders—Deut. 28:27
Slavery
Spirit of death—Deut. 28:53
Torment—Matt. 4:24; Luke 16:28
Tourette syndrome
Ulcers—Deut. 28:27; Luke 16:20
Unforgiveness
Venereal disease—Ps. 38
Weakness, chronic—Luke 13:11; John 5:5
Wounded spirit—Lev. 26:16; Prov. 18:14

Note: *For oppression, also see "Spirit of Heaviness."

BIND	LOOSE
‣ Spirit of infirmity—Luke 13:11; Prov. 18:14	‣ Wholeness—Matt. 6:22; 9:22 ‣ Health—3 John 2; Jer. 33:6

SPIRIT OF JEALOUSY

Accusations—1 Tim. 5:19
Anger—Gen. 4:5-6; Prov. 6:34; 14:29; 22:24-25; 29:22-23
Argumentative
Backbiting—Prov. 19:5
Belittling
Bickering—1 Tim. 6:4
Bitterness—Prov. 18:19
Blasphemy
Burn—Ps. 79:5
Causing divisions
Coarse jesting (inappropriate/ dishonorable words)—Eph. 5:4

Competitive, excessively—Gen. 4:4-5
Contentious—Prov. 13:10
Covetousness—1 Tim. 6:10
Critical
Cruelty—Prov. 27:4; Song of Sol. 8:6
Cry, inability to
Cursing—Prov. 18:21
Debates, seeking to cause
Deception—1 Tim. 6:5
Destruction—Job 26:6
Discontent—1 Tim. 5:13
Disputes—Job 23:7

Dissatisfaction
Distrust
Divisions, causing—Gal. 5:19
Dreamer
Enmity—Rom. 8:7
Envy—Gen. 21:9
Factiousness
Faultfinding
Fighting—Ps. 56:1
Gangs
Gossip
Greed—Prov. 15:27
Hardness of heart—James 1:14; 1
   Tim. 4:1
Hatred—Gen. 3; 7:3–4, 8; 1 Thess.
   4:8
Hurt
Indifference
Inferiority
Insecurity
Judging
Lying—1 Tim. 4:1; Prov. 12:22
Malice—Prov. 4:16–17
Materialism—Ps. 30:6

Mocking—Jer. 15:17–18
Murder—Gen. 4:8
Quarrelling—Col. 3:13
Rage—Prov. 6:34
Rebellion—Deut. 21:18
Restlessness
Retaliation
Revenge—Prov. 6:34; 14:16–17
Sadism
Self-centeredness—Luke 18:11
Self-hatred
Selfishness—2 Peter 2:10
Slander—Prov. 10:18
Spite—Prov. 6:34; 14:16–17
Stealing
Strife—Prov. 10:12
Suicide—Acts 1:18
Suspicion
Temper—Prov. 6:34
Unforgiveness
Unworthiness
Violence—Prov. 16:29
Wickedness—Prov. 3:31

BIND	LOOSE
➤ Spirit of jealousy—Num. 5:14, 30; Ezek. 8:3	➤ Love—1 Peter 1:22; Gal. 5:22; Prov. 10:12

SPIRIT OF PERVERSION/WHOREDOM

Abortion
Adultery—Ezra 16:15, 28; Prov.
   5:1–14
Adulterous fantasy—Prov. 12:26
Arrogance—Rom. 1:29–31
Atheism—Prov. 14:2; Rom. 1:30
Bastard (unholy covenant)—Deut.
   23:2; Zech. 9:6
Bisexuality
Child abuse

Confusion (spirit of Egypt)—Isa.
   19:3
Contentious—Rom. 1:29; Phil. 2:14–
   16; 1 Tim. 6:4–5; Titus 3:10–11
Crankiness
Cruelty—Ps. 74:20
Deception—Prov. 28:18; Rom.
   1:30–31
Dissatisfaction, chronic
Diviner—Hosea 4:12

Dizziness—Isa. 19:14

Doctrinal error (twisting the Word)

Doubt—Deut. 28:66

Drunkard—Prov. 23:21

Emotional dissatisfaction

Emotional weakness

Excessive activity

Exhibitionism

Evil actions—Prov. 17:20, 23

False teachings—Mark 13:22; 2 Tim. 3:13; Deut. 13:6–8

Fantasies (lustful)

Filthy-mindedness—Prov. 2:12; 23:33

Foolishness—Prov. 1:22; 19:1

Fornication—Hosea 4:13–19; Rom. 1:29; Heb. 13:14

Frigidity

Greed—Prov. 22:22

Guilt

Harlotry—Prov. 23:27–28

Hatred—Ps. 139:22; Prov. 26:26

Hoarding

Homosexuality—Gen. 19:4–7; Rom. 1:27

Idolatry—Hosea 4:12; Ezek. 16

Illegitimate children—Gen. 19:36–38

Incest—Gen. 19:31–33

Incubus and Succubus—Gen. 6:2–4

Lesbianism—Rom. 1:26

Love of power—Job 2:6; Ps. 10:15; Lam. 5:8

Lust for: authority, body (sexual), food, money (Prov. 15:27; 1 Tim. 6:7–14), position, perverse sexual acts, power, sex, social standing, the world, worldliness

Lust (all kinds)—Prov. 23:31–35

Marking, cutting, or tattoos—Lev. 19:28

Masturbation

Pedophilia—Lev. 19:29

Pornography

Poverty—Lev. 26:18–20

Prostitution (of spirit, soul, or body)—Prov. 5:1–14; 22:14

Rape—2 Sam. 13:1–14

Sadomasochism

Seduction—1 Tim. 4:1; 2 Tim. 3:13; Prov. 1:10

Self-exposure

Self-gratification—Prov. 5:3–6

Self, lover of—Prov. 4:24

Sensuality—Jude 19

Sexual deviation—Gen. 19:8

Sexual dissatisfaction—Ezek. 16:28

Sexual perversion—Rom. 1:17–32; 2 Tim. 3:2

Sexual sin, all—Jude 7–8

Shame—Ps. 44:15

Stubbornness

Sodomy—Gen. 19:5; Jude 7

Transvestite

Unbelief—Matt. 13:58

Uncontrollable sexual desires—1 Cor. 6:13–16; Phil. 3:19

Unfaithfulness—Prov. 5:2–14; Ezek. 16:15, 28

Weakness—Gen. 38:15–18

Whoredom—Hosea 3:12–14

Worldliness—James 4:4

Worry, chronic—Prov. 19:3; Job 30:27

Wounded spirit—Prov. 15:4

BIND	LOOSE
‣ Spirit of perversion—Isa. 19:14; Rom. 1:17–32 ‣ Spirit of whoredom—Lev. 19:29; Ezek. 16:28–29; Isa. 19:14; Hosea 4:12; 5:4; Jer. 3:9	‣ Chastity—1 Pet. 3:2; 2 Cor. 11:2 ‣ Discernment—Job 6:30; Ezek. 44:23; Heb. 5:14 ‣ Godliness—1 Tim. 4:8; 2 Pet. 3:11 ‣ Purity—1 Tim. 4:12

SPIRIT OF SLUMBER/UNBELIEF

ADD
ADHD
Blasphemer—2 Tim. 3:2
Blind—Rom. 2:19–20
Can't hear the Word of God
Can't stay awake in church—Rom. 13:11–12
Confusion—Job 10:15
Distracted easily—Ps. 88:15
Dizziness—James 3:16
Fear—1 John 4:18
Lazy—Prov. 19:15
Lethargy
Mental slowness

Perversions
Sickness:* anemia, arthritis (Prov. 12:4; 14:30), asthma, circulatory problems, chronic fatigue syndrome, eye disorders (Rev. 3:18), hearing problems (dull of hearing; Matt. 13:13–14), palpitations
Sleepiness—Job 33:15
Sleeplessness—Prov. 4:16
Terror—Job 31:23
Torment—1 John 4:18
Unbelief—Heb. 3:12

Notes: *For sickness, also see "Spirit of Infirmity."

BIND	LOOSE
‣ Spirit of unbelief, stupor, or slumber—Rom. 11:8; Isa. 6:9; Matt. 13:14	‣ Being filled with the Spirit—Acts 2:4; Eph. 5:18 ‣ Opened eyes—John 9:30; Ps. 119:18

Notes

Introduction

1. Laurie Goodstein, "Evangelicals Fear the Loss of Teenagers," *New York Times*, October 6, 2006, http://www.nytimes .com/2006/10/06/us/06evangelical.html?pagewanted=print (accessed May 19, 2011).

Chapter 1—Demons Really Want to Harm My Child?

1. Teen Mania, "Teen Trends," http://www.teenmania.com/index.cfm/ PageID/1686/index.html (accessed May 19, 2011).

Chapter 3—Whose Demon Is It?

1. Albert Pike, *Morals and Dogma of the Ancient and Accepted Scottish Rite of Freemasonry* (Charleston: L. H. Jenkins, Inc., 1871), 435.
2. Steve Goodier, "Love the Children," BestInspiration.com, http:// www.bestinspiration.com/stories/Love_the_Children.htm (accessed May 20, 2011).

Chapter 4—The Lure of Worldly Influences

1. Teen Mania, "Teen Trends."
2. Ibid.
3. American Academy of Pediatrics, "AAP Advocates for Safer Media and Music Lyrics," news release, October 19, 2009, http://www .aap.org/advocacy/releases/nce09musiclyrics.htm (accessed May 20, 2011).
4. Keren Eyal et al., "Sexual Socialization Messages on Television Programs Most Popular Among Teens (Report)," *Journal of*

Broadcasting and Electronic Media (June 1, 2007), http://www
.highbeam.com/doc/1G1-167695497.html (accessed May 20, 2011).

5. Elizabeth Mary Gabzdyl, "Contraceptive Care of Adolescents:
   Overview, Tips, Strategies, and Implications for Student Nurses,"
   Journal of School Nursing 26, no. 4 (August 2010): http://jsn.sagepub
   .com/content/26/4/267.abstract (accessed May 20, 2011).

6. Planned Parenthood of Southeastern Virginia, "May Is National
   Teen Pregnancy Prevention Month," http://www.ppsev.org/media/
   documents/Teenpregnancypreventionarticle.pdf (accessed May 20,
   2011).

7. BBC.co.uk, "Bookclub: J. K. Rowling Interview," BBC Radio 4,
   August 1, 1999, http://www.bbc.co.uk/iplayer/episode/p00fpv7t/
   Bookclub_J_K_Rowling/ (accessed May 20, 2011), transcript
   viewed at http://www.angelfire.com/mi3/cookarama/bbcintaug99
   .html (accessed May 20, 2011).

8. Angelfire.com, "Yahooligans Chat With J. K. Rowling, Part 2,"
   October 20, 2000, http://www.angelfire.com/mi3/cookarama/
   yahoolintoct00pt2.html (accessed May 20, 2011).

9. Interview with J. K. Rowling, Edinburgh Book Festival, Sunday,
   August 15, 2004, http://harrypotter.bloomsbury.com/author/
   interviews/individual1 (accessed May 20, 2011).

10. Austin Cline, "Does Harry Potter Promote Wicca or Witchcraft? Is
    Harry Potter a Pagan Book?," About.com, http://atheism.about
    .com/od/harrypotter/i/witchcraft_2.htm (accessed May 20, 2011).

11. BBCNews, "Harry Potter Finale Sales Hit 11M," July 23, 2007,
    http://news.bbc.co.uk/2/hi/entertainment/6912529.stm (accessed
    May 20, 2011).

12. Ibid.

13. Box Office Mojo, "Worldwide Grosses," http://www.boxofficemojo
    .com/alltime/world/ (accessed May 20, 2011).

14. BBCNews, "JK Rowling 'Richer Than Queen,'" April 27, 2003,
    http://news.bbc.co.uk/2/hi/uk_news/2979033.stm (accessed May
    20, 2011). BusinessWeek.com, "Harry Potter Brand Wizard," July
    18, 2005, http://www.businessweek.com/innovate/content/jul2005/
    di20050721_060250.htm (accessed May 20, 2011).

15. The Official Website of Stephenie Meyer, "The Story Behind *Twilight*," http://www.stepheniemeyer.com/twilight.html (accessed May 23, 2011).

16. The Official Website of Stephenie Meyer, "Twilight Series: What's with the apple?," http://www.stepheniemeyer.com/twilight_faq .html#apple (accessed May 23, 2011).

17. As quoted in bfwebster, "Finally: Some Evangelical Criticism of 'Twilight,'" *Adventures in Mormonism* (blog), January 23, 2009, http://www.nothingwavering.org/post/8293/2009-01-23/finally -some-evangelical-criticism-of-twilight.html (accessed May 23, 2011).

18. Ibid.

19. Wikipedia.org, s.v. "*Twilight* (novel)," http://en.wikipedia.org/wiki/ Twilight_(novel) (accessed May 23, 2011).

20. "Marketwatch—Twilight Statistics," November 20, 2008, http:// twilightersanonymous.com/market-watch-twilight-statistics.html (accessed May 23, 2011).

21. Melissa Maerz, "Hot Actor: Q&A With 'Twilight' Star Robert Pattinson," *Rolling Stone*, December 11, 2008, http://www .rollingstone.com/movies/news/hot-actor-q-a-with-twilight-star -robert-pattinson-20081211 (accessed May 23, 2011).

22. As quoted in bfwebster, "Finally: Some Evangelical Criticism of 'Twilight.'"

23. Cindy Jacobs, *Deliver Us From Evil* (Ventura, CA: Regal Books, 2001), 70.

24. Barna.org, "Barna Lists the 12 Most Significant Religious Findings," December 20, 2006, http://www.barna.org/barna-update/article/12 -faithspirituality/141-barna-lists-the-12-most-significant-religious -findings (accessed May 23, 2011).

25. Barna.org, "New Research Explores Teenage Views and Behavior Regarding the Supernatural," January 23, 2006, http://www.barna .org/barna-update/article/5-barna-update/164-new-research -explores-teenage-views-and-behavior-regarding-the-supernatural (accessed May 23, 2011).

26. As quoted in video by Chris Wilson, http://www.vidmax.com/ video/2604/Imagine_hanging_from_hooks_dug_into_

your_back___45__that__39_s_what_these_guys_do_all_day/ (accessed October 10, 2010).

27. Ibid.

28. Ibid.

29. Craig A. Anderson and Karen E. Dill, "Video Games and Aggressive Thoughts, Feelings, and Behaviors in the Laboratory and in Life," *Journal of Personality and Social Psychology* 78, no. 4 (April 2000): 772–790.

30. American Academy of Pediatrics, "AAP Advocates for Safer Media and Music Lyrics."

31. Victor C. Strasburger, "Children, Adolescents, and the Media," *Current Problems in Pediatric and Adolescent Health Care* 34, no. 2 (February 2004): 54–113, http://www.sfu.ca/~wchane/sa304articles/Strasburger.pdf (accessed May 23, 2011).

32. Ibid.

33. George A. Mathers and Larry A. Nichols, *Dictionary of Cults, Sects, Religions and the Occult* (Grand Rapids, MI: Zondervan, 1993), 182.

34. Kirsten Orsini-Meinhard, "Yoga Industry Gains Strength," http://www.bikramyoga.com/News/TheColoradoan071005.php (accessed November 3, 2010).

35. Barna.org, "New Research Explores Teenage Views and Behavior Regarding the Supernatural."

36. Ibid.

Chapter 5—The Truth Behind Peer Pressure

1. David B. Guralink, *Webster's New World Dictionary* (Cleveland, OH: Simon and Schuster, 1982), s.v. "pressure."

2. Dictionary.com, s.v. "peer pressure," Dictionary.com Unabridged, Random House, Inc., http://dictionary.reference.com/browse/peer pressure (accessed May 23, 2011).

3. Teen Mania, "Teen Trends."

4. National School Safety and Security Services, "Gangs and School Safety," http://www.schoolsecurity.org/trends/gangs.html (accessed May 23, 2011).

5. "Adolescents and Peer Pressure: Interviews," http://sitemaker.umich .edu/356.darnell/interviews (accessed May 5, 2011). Publisher's note: We have been unsuccessful in contacting the owner of this site to request permission to use. If you have any information on contacting the owner of this site, please contact us to pass on that information. Thank you.

6. Centers for Disease Control and Prevention, *Youth Risk Behavior Surveillance—United States, 2009*, Surveillance Summaries, June 4, 2010, *MMWR* 59, no. SS-5, http://www.cdc.gov/mmwr/pdf/ss/ ss5905.pdf (accessed May 23, 2011).

Chapter 6—The Tragedy of Abuse

1. ChildHelp.org, "National Child Abuse Statistics," http://www .childhelp.org/pages/statistics#abuse-conseq (accessed May 23, 2011).

2. Administration for Children and Families, "About Human Trafficking," US Department of Health and Human Services, http://www.acf.hhs.gov/trafficking/about/index.html (accessed May 23, 2011).

3. Andrew Cockburn, "21st-Century Slaves," NationalGeographic.com, http://ngm.nationalgeographic.com/ngm/0309/feature1/index .html#biblio (accessed May 23, 2011).

4. US Department of State, "Introduction," *Trafficking in Persons Report*, June 3, 2005, http://www.state.gov/g/tip/rls/ tiprpt/2005/46606.htm (accessed May 23, 2011).

5. US Department of State, *Trafficking in Persons Report*, June 2008, 7, http://www.state.gov/documents/organization/105501.pdf (accessed May 23, 2011).

6. United Nations, "Press Conference on Human Trafficking by Executive Director of United Nations Office on Drugs and Crime," May 13, 2009, http://www.un.org/News/briefings/ docs/2009/090513_UNODC.doc.htm (accessed May 23, 2011).

7. Kristin Collins and Aimee Grace, "Human Trafficking and Healthcare: Modern-Day Slavery and Its Effects on the Health of Teens and Children in the US," August 12, 2009, http://peds .stanford.edu/Tools/documents/human_traficking.pdf (accessed May 23, 2011).

8. Brad Stone, "Sex Ads Seen Adding Revenue to Craigslist," *New York Times*, April 12, 2010, http://www.nytimes.com/2010/04/26/ technology/26craigslist.html (accessed September 25, 2010).

9. US Department of State, "Trafficking Victims Protection Reauthorization Act of 2005," January 10, 2006, http://www.state .gov/g/tip/laws/61106.htm (accessed May 23, 2011).

10. Kevin Bales and Ron Soodalter, *The Slave Next Door: Human Trafficking and Slavery in America Today* (Los Angeles: University of California Press, Ltd., 2009), 7.

11. Library of Congress, "111th Congress, 1st Session: S. 2925," December 22, 2009, http://thomas.loc.gov/home/gpoxmlc111/ s2925_is.xml (accessed May 23, 2011).

12. US Department of Justice, "Domestic Sex Trafficking of Minors," http://www.justice.gov/criminal/ceos/prostitution.html (accessed May 23, 2011).

13. Traffick911.com, "Innocence Taken," http://www.traffick911.com/ page/what-is-human-trafficking (accessed May 23, 2011).

14. Kelli Stevens et al., *Domestic Minor Sex Trafficking: Ft. Worth, Texas* (Springfield, VA: PIP Printing, 2008), 7.

15. Ibid.

16. WOWT.com, "Porn Bust Stuns Neighbors," December 18, 2004, http://www.wowt.com/news/headlines/1300876.html (accessed May 23, 2011). Jim Longworth, "Child Porn Download Case Is Obscene," YesWeekly.com, December 16, 2009, http://www.yesweekly.com/ triad/article-8103-child-porn-download-case-is-obscene.html (accessed May 23, 2011).

17. Rob Winters, *The Elisha Commission* (Phoenix, AZ: Gatekeepers International Prophetic Network, Inc., n.d.), 16.

18. Ibid.

19. Enough.org, "Archive of Statistics on Internet Dangers: Internet Pornography," http://www.enough.org/inside.php?tag=stat%20 archives (accessed May 23, 2011).

20. Enough.org, "Child Pornography," http://www.enough.org/inside .php?tag=stat%20archives#3 (accessed May 23, 2011).

21. Winters, *The Elisha Commission*, 16.

22. BeautyFromAshes.org, "Porn Statistics," http://www .beautyfromashes.org/contentpages.aspx?parentnavigationid=10396& viewcontentpageguid=4cda8536-69d2-45cb-bbd4-6955e9432e0c (accessed May 23, 2011).

23. Winters, *The Elisha Commission*, 16.

24. Ibid.

25. Ibid.

26. CouncilIdaho.net, "The Defenders," http://councilidaho.net/features .aspx?region=31467&ContentID=47662 (accessed May 23, 2011).

27. As quoted by Sergeant Chris Bray, Phoenix, AZ, Police Department.

28. Alice Smith, *Beyond the Lie* (Bloomington, MN: Bethany House Publishers, 2006), 39–40.

Chapter 7—The Power of Trauma

1. Thomas Verny with John Kelly, *The Secret Life of the Unborn Child* (New York: Dell Publishing, 1981), 12–13.

2. Jane Lindstrom, "Tommy's Essay," *Condensed Chicken Soup for the Soul* (Deerfield Beach, FL: HCI, 1996), as quoted on http:// www.inspirationalstories.com/2/224.html (accessed May 5, 2011). Permission has been requested from publisher to reprint.

Chapter 8—Words Will Never Hurt Me?

1. BullyingStatistics.org, "School Bullying," http://www .bullyingstatistics.org/content/school-bullying.html (accessed May 24, 2011).

2. Ibid.

3. Anthony Frazier, "Bullying, the Art of Killing the Human Spirit," IndianaGazette.com, November 30, 2010, http://www .indianagazette.com/article_5079b7e7-2bbb-5bbe-84dd -4a3cbe950532.html (accessed May 24, 2011).

4. "Bullying Statistics," http://www.pascack.k12.nj.us/70271919141818/ lib/70271919141818/Bullying_Statistics.htm (accessed May 24, 2011).

5. Ibid.

6. Ibid.

7. Megan Gordan, "Arizona School Officials Address Bullying," *Arizona Republic*, April 25, 2010, http://www.azcentral.com/ news/articles/2010/04/25/20100425-school-bullying-arizona.html (accessed May 24, 2011).

8. "Bullying Statistics."

9. Ibid.

10. Ibid.

11. Ibid.

12. Ibid.

13. Ibid.

14. Values.com, "A Guy Who Gets Consistently Bullied," http://www .values.com/your-inspirational-stories?page=18 (accessed May 24, 2011).

15. Teen Mania, "Teen Trends."

16. Larry K. Brown, Christopher D. Houck, Wendy S. Hadley, and Celia M. Lescano, "Self-Cutting and Sexual Risk Among Adolescents in Intensive Psychiatric Treatment," *Psychiatric Services* 56 (February 2005): 216–218, http://psychservices.psychiatryonline .org/cgi/content/full/56/2/216 (accessed May 24, 2011).

17. Ibid.

18. Ibid.

19. As quoted in seamist, "Teen Cutting: Understanding Why," *HubPages* (blog), http://hubpages.com/hub/understanding-teenager

-behavior-adolescent-self-injury-teens-cutting (accessed May 24, 2011).

20. Ibid.

21. DiscoveryHealth.com writers, "Teens in Crisis: Cutting on the Rise," http://health.howstuffworks.com/pregnancy-and-parenting/teenage -health/cutting-on-the-rise.htm (accessed May 24, 2011).

22. Jennifer Radcliffe, "Self-Destructive 'Cutters' Living Their Lives on the Edge," *Los Angeles Daily News*, March 29, 2004, viewed at http://www.jenniferboyer.com/sinews9-1.htm (accessed May 24, 2011).

23. ScottCounseling.com, "Self-Injury Behavior," (blog), February 6, 2009, http://www.scottcounseling.com/wordpress/cutting-self -injury-facts-statistics/2009/02/06/ (accessed May 24, 2011).

24. Jane E. Brody, "The Growing Wave of Teenage Self-Injury," *New York Times*, May 6, 2008, http://www.nytimes.com/2008/05/06/ health/06brod.html (accessed May 24, 2011).

25. seamist, "Teen Cutting: Understanding Why."

26. Teen Mania, "Teen Trends."

27. Uncyclopedia.com, s.v. "Emo Kid," http://uncyclopedia.wikia.com/ wiki/Emo_kid (accessed May 24, 2011).

28. Alice Smith, *Delivering the Captives* (Bloomington, MN: Bethany House Publishers, 2006), 112–113.

Chapter 9—The Power of Affirmation

1. James Dobson, "Routine Whining Can Be Eliminated by Ignoring It," ChristianIndex.org, September 24, 2009, http://www .christianindex.org/5854.article (accessed May 24, 2011).

2. Smith, *Beyond the Lie*, 111–112.

3. Ras and Bev Robinson, *Convergence of Quantum Physics, Scripture and Prophecy* (Peoria, IL: Intermedia Publishing Group, Inc., 2009), 29–30.

Chapter 12—Turning the Hearts of the Fathers to the
Children and the Hearts of the Children to the Fathers

1. Warren Wiersbe, *The Bible Exposition Commentary*, Libronix Digital
Library System, LBS Series X, Disc B (1.1a).

Appendix—Apparent Demonic Groupings List

1. Smith, *Delivering the Captives*, 96–118. Used by permission of
publisher.